S0-CFK-212

WRITING:

What's Good, Bad and Ugly

D.G. Wilkes

Abbey Isle Publishing
Printed in Victoria, Canada

Copyright 2007 © Donald G. Wilkes
All rights reserved
No portion of this book may be reproduced
or transmitted in any form or means whatsoever,
excepting short passages for review, without the
prior permission in writing from the publisher.

Library and Archives Canada Cataloguing in Publication
Gordon, Donald, 1935-
Writing : what's good, bad and ugly / D.G. Wilkes.
ISBN 978-0-9737633-2-4
1. Authorship. I. Title.
PN147.G65 2007 808'.02   C2007-905141-3

Content of this book is intended to
provide some information and encourage
readers to explore other avenues or sources
for writing assistance. Readers are solely
responsible for interpretation, use or
misuse of material contained
within these pages.

Contact: tradon@islandnet.com

What you'll find in the following pages:

Notes:

If you expect others to be attracted to your work, what you write must first matter to you. A lot! A fiction creation should produce word pictures, tantalising images, if you expect to entice potential book buyers. A non-fiction offering must deliver insight or something fresh on a topic. There are oodles of books out there, each competing for attention, attempting to grab passing readers and entice them into digging out cash or plastic.

While it's important to do what's right and proper to launch a good, hopefully successful book, do try to think outside the box (as some say). Seek to differ. Don't accept, assume, that first idea that comes to mind. Rethink the matter. For instance, in designing this cover, with little thought given to the issue, I adopted black print—then one morning, pondering how I might improve the ensemble, *brown* popped into my head: darker brown words against a darker beige and textured or fibered background.

To lessen initial brain drain and invested research time, at first work with what's familiar or comfortable. Also, early in the game, be prepared to accept that what you ultimately produce may end up middling, despite your best effort. Everyone can't be a winner, a leading light, and *middling* is better than *mediocre* or material even less appealing.

Dedicated hard work breeds improvement. Perseverance and becoming better known generates success. And, do bear in mind that getting things done usually takes more time than expected—plan ahead with that in mind.

A writer inclined toward fiction must shift mindset to tackle non-fiction. For the latter, in addition to the basic components that apply to both, unless help is at hand, (s)he must be prepared to assemble all that produces a hopefully successful outcome. Research and analysis. Material organisation. Formatted presentation in a clear and meaningful fashion.

I guess that's why I lean toward fiction, since the only factual topics with which I'm sufficiently familiar, that readily come to mind, are travel, politics as entertainment, wine and the meaning and interplay of words.

As for wine, I cannot claim to be an expert (has been defined as an old drip under pressure) but I've long been a devotee and I did manage to get published an article: *Confessions Of A Wine Slob*. Unfortunately advancing age and acid reflux has all but put paid to my enjoyment of that elixir of the gods found in bottles. But I'm not complaining. Through the years I've had my fair share—that attested to by numerous corks once strung together and hung in a cottage near Haliburton in Ontario.

An ambition never achieved: To live on a Greek island, dine on Italian food and gracefully quaff some Margaux or a fine red wine from the environs of Beaune or Nuits-St-Georges in France.

In some ways I wish I could manage a serious interest in politics but unfortunately, or perhaps fortunately, I just find it darned entertaining, a performance filled with drama exceeding what's offered by the best of soap operas found on television. That attitude resulted in an article that focused on one political convention.

No pain, no gain; no risk, no reward. Saying you want to be a writer or occasionally adding a few words to a file or page that seldom moves forward, is not the same as actually sitting down and investing the necessary devotion, diligence, time and effort needed to master sizeable chunks of a project and commit to file or paper what's long been eating away at you and awaiting disclosure.

Getting published is a gratifying event that provides a rush, in particular the first time your material appears in print. No matter what success follows, you'll not forget seeing that first successful effort on a page printed by someone else. I never have.

After a measure of writing success, try to escape from the pack, albeit modestly at first. Venture into the unknown and stretch your boundaries. Consider writers in the past who have shunned the tried and true to whatever extent in favour of pursuing an alternate path. How did they fare? Who followed their lead? Why not you?

As a writer, you should never leave home without pad and pen. Ideas can pop up at the oddest times, may be lost forever if not immediately recorded. Some of my best thoughts arise when I'm out walking. Lacking decent penmanship, when I get back home I quickly transcribe what was scribbled on the back of a recycled business card. Those readable scraps of paper are then set beside the computer or, if for future use, pinned to an adjacent bulletin board or slipped into a designated file folder. Having failed to transcribe on occasion, if the note was ever deciphered, it took me days to determine the content.

Few scribes make a living writing and most would starve if not for day-job earnings. With the abundant influx of books from below the border, too few people buy Canadian creations. With an average annual income from writing said to be somewhere around five thousand dollars, many folk writing seriously make little more than ten thousand dollars a year.

For those who opt for self-publishing, by whatever means, the return on considerable invested effort may produce little more than a partial recovery of dollars spent. Nowadays that scenario only worsens as a greater number of writers strive to produce something that hopefully might become a Canadian bestseller (five thousand copies?). More fortunate scribes manage to gain entry into the huge U.S. market.

For wannabe writers, and those achieving a measure of success without attempting to make a living at it, getting an article or book into print could be considered a costly and frustrating yet gratifying ego trip—one often fraught with disappointment. If you do give it a go, be prepared to accept and deal with rejection or, more likely, receiving no response at all.

An innovative query letter or email, including a quality-writing sample, has a better chance of getting a positive response. But don't contact one recipient at a time. Use a shotgun approach. If by chance you get more than one response I'm sure you'll find a way to handle that problem.

Rejection has knocked off hordes of struggling writers who decided that their best efforts were wasted, that they'd had enough and couldn't take it any more. During the publication-seeking process don't get your hopes up too high. Be patient and be prepared to wait (months, not years) for what may never arrive. Editors and publishers at best are slow to respond, but bear in mind that you are only one of a host of hopefuls chasing the same dream. While awaiting a response, start or work on another project.

To get a better idea of the writing process, what's going on and what to expect, consider attending a writing workshop or a gathering like the well-attended Surrey International Writers' Conference, held in British Columbia each fall. Meet other writers, both seasoned and novices, those hopeful and those already successful. Encounter differing perspectives. Join assorted sessions. Hopefully, the experience will give you a better idea of what lies ahead.

Get an assessment of your writing efforts. Perhaps, as some have, you just might get lucky and connect with a publisher. I know someone who attended the Surrey gathering and ended up signing a three-book deal with an American publisher.

How about joining a writing group, in person or online and getting a better idea of how your material might fit into the world of printed pages? How it may be received. While some writing groups are more casual in nature, more social than serious, others focus on critiquing material presented. And, critiquing isn't criticism. It's constructive comment and suggestions offered in the interest of helping a writer improve her or his material. If critiquing, to encourage acceptance of any following negative comment, it's best to start with a positive observation.

Given the option or inclination, you might want to try writing some non-fiction before attempting to find a home for a fictional article or book. Non-fiction appears easier to sell and receiving a bit of writing income might bolster ambition and enthusiasm, ease the frustration that accompanies days spent writing and later trying to flog, find a home for, unappreciated material.

While some folk persist with pen and paper or a typewriter, most seriously hopeful and successful scribes have adopted a computer as the preferred means of assembling their work. Given its popularity and my use of the program, references in this book relate to Microsoft Word, a wordprocessor that replaced my trusty older version of WordStar, a program I'd used for almost two decades, had long refused to abandon. But even luddites eventually wake up, get the message and do what's needed, the right thing.

If you use a computer, do you consistently save and backup created or altered files? If not, why not? The time taken to copy files to a floppy, CD, DVD or USB/flash drive is miniscule compared to the hours you'll have to invest to recreate lost files. Things do go wrong. For instance, say you are working on a file and you encounter a glitch from which you cannot escape. Or, heaven forbid, you could experience a system crash or a power failure. Work interrupted or at a stop, with a recent save or backup you can return to what existed before trouble arrived. Comfort beats anxiety.

Despite shortcomings, a laptop/notebook computer can prove handy for a writer, particularly if more than one workplace is involved. Some people like to write while slumped into a comfortable chair, computer perched on lap (thus: 'laptop'). Others lack sufficient living space to set up a desktop computer. Notebooks are also handy for displaying material to others on their premises.

A few decades ago I worked on a textbook project with a short timeframe. Rather than stay home and miss quality cottage time, I took my laptop along and worked mornings in the country. Nowadays I use a reasonably new desktop, along with two printers: an aged and quirky laser that produces great black print, a newer inkjet that can also produce colour output. A doddery old dot matrix that was great for printing drafts bit the dust mere months ago.

With writing, some measure of research is usually essential. Libraries and books can be helpful but online searching provides quick and easy access to scads of information. While the internet does contain debatable material, it's a veritable cornucopia of helpful facts and figures and is seldom a waste of search time invested.

Most writing pundits disparage clichés. While I agree that they should be severely scrutinised and curtailed, be used with discretion, at time they're just the cup of tea, a great fit for the context. I use a few and adapt others.

Working on this book I had no wish to duplicate what's better sought from a dictionary or assorted tomes on grammar but I'd be remiss if I didn't mention, from time to time, items that ever seem to plague writers, a few of which I've struggled with for years; for example, the proper use of *who* and *whom*.

Writing: What's Good, Bad and Ugly, focusing by section on specific aspects of the writing process, is the result of considerable searching, writing attempts and varying experiences accumulated through the years. Not intended to be an erudite dissertation on the art of writing, the intention or hope is that the content, intended to be practical and realistic in nature, will spark thought and trigger ideas, will nudge a writer into exploring other writing avenues and books focusing on particular aspects of writing found confusing or elusive. Hopefully what's offered in these pages will induce writers to strive to convert ugly/bad into better/best.

The English language evolves. Some words and phrases suitable yesterday have become optional or no longer serve the original purpose. Not to be overdone, ending a sentence with a preposition (...disposed of.) is now acceptable, in some circles or circumstances. English or American usage? Organize or organise? Scrutinize or scrutinise? As a result of that dilemma, I expect you'll find both 'z' and 's' used in such words in this book.

More weird still sounds better than *weirder* but *quieter* works as well or better than *more quiet*. While other language shifts may grate, few equate to using *less* where *fewer* (countable) is proper or improperly substituting *quantity* for *number* (countable). When I hear those two I still grind my teeth and struggle to keep silent.

A word about copyright: How you express what you write about is automatically protected by copyright as committed to file or paper—but not so for ideas or a title. If concerned about copyright security and prepared to invest the funds, send a manuscript copy by registered mail to your address and leave the envelope unopened.

While *author* may better apply to the source of what's written, in this book that term is used interchangeably with *writer*, with a few *scribes* thrown in here and there for variety.

I seldom mark the pages of books I read but, with intended helpmates like this—books aimed at stimulating thought, encouraging exploration and offering assistance—I don't hesitate to put a highlighter to work and scribble notes aside particular paragraphs.

Early on, working on this book I discovered a tendency to repeat some comments. Attempting to avoid doing that, I then realised that some items are best repeated so that they wouldn't get overlooked, passed over too lightly. If you note instances where I've gone overboard with debatable justification, my apologies...

Words Galore

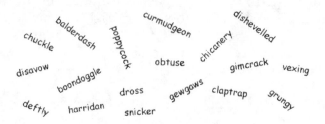

Writers are frequently eager readers, lovers of words. Or they should be. Often what they read for pleasure yields handy prompts: an unknown word, a catchy phrase, a unique or stylish descriptive approach, a story idea or plot twist. While it's verboten to lift in its entirety what you like from what you read, adapting what's discovered for use in another form is frequently done. There are few new story themes, ideas or plots. Much of what we read is similar to what's been written before, often many times over. The treatment is what makes content appear different.

With writing, nothing is more important than those chosen words that end up on paper as a result of initial inspiration and subsequent revision and polishing. How words are used develops style, a way of writing that hopefully will elevate an effort above that of others, distinguish the results and make them appealing to readers. Search out richer words, nouns or verbs that can stand alone, without being propped up by trite adjectives or adverbs. Avoid flimsy words like *interesting* or *pretty.* Instead, use *captivating* or *gorgeous;* they sound better and are more descriptive.

To achieve superior writing you must respect the use of words and relish the time frequently devoted to delving into a dictionary or thesaurus in search of that word best suited for the job, the one that will notably improve the material. While usually helpful and worth noting, don't depend upon a wordprocessor's spelling or grammar checker. Those prompts are based upon a program's set of rules, judgements that may not fit the language or context under review. Check elsewhere; consult hardcopy. Computer-based assessors are seldom as good, as comprehensive, as what can be found in a hefty reference book.

Which English to adopt: British, American or Canadian, the latter having absorbed words and meanings from the other two? Color or colour. Words ending with 'er' or 're.' Program or programme.

The decision could depend upon where you hope or expect to sell your work. However, settling for Canadian and accepting some American usage, there are language differences that should be avoided, such as using *good* where *well* is proper. The latter usually means a degree of health or success: He's doing good - no. He's doing well - yes.

And then there's capitalisation. When yes, when no? There are conventions, such as 'North' for an area and 'north' for direction. Do unneeded capitalised words in a sentence add clutter? Relative to computerland: Web or web, Net or net, Cyberspace or cyberspace, Email or email, Internet or internet.

Email has lost its capitalisation; do others persist? Anyway, relative to the internet I've chosen to use lower case for such words.

To become a better writer you need to treasure and accumulate new words, read books that favour good writing. If you spot a word you don't know or might be able to use to advantage, put that (pristine?) dictionary to work. Look up the word and perhaps record it for later consideration. To use a particular word to advantage, consider the sound and rhythm of words that will be adjacent to the selected one.

Need something to read while travelling? Take along and browse a pocket-sized dictionary or thesaurus, perhaps with a highlighter in hand. A sampling of good words: snarl, underbelly, blather, ergo, grew apace, dross, boondoggle, disavow, popinjay, claptrap.

While formal English has its place within the field of non-fiction, most writers of fiction adopt a more casual approach to what they commit to paper. Appropriate diction—choice and use of words—adds tone and style, assists in reaching those all-important readers. Avoid overworked words but do employ those that readily come to mind and are widely understood, foot soldiers that have performed well through the years.

Tone emanates from the words a writer chooses to express attitude or inclination, how she or he reacts to a subject, hopes to involve a reader. Concrete words, clarity and a measure of introduced sound are what's wanted, not a flat and dull delivery of text. Why just say, 'He advised the group of his objections.' when you could say, 'He stunned the foursome seated upfront and stirred a previously bored audience with his grasp of the topic.'

In choosing words for what you write, bear in mind the reading level of the anticipated audience. For fiction you'll need to aim lower than for non-fiction. In short, simplicity works best. Smaller words are more effective than bigger ones. Using a few more obscure words might be tempting but do so with care and in moderation. Much of what's written nowadays targets a grade eight level, or lower.

I'm not sure what's available for today's Microsoft Windows but back in DOS days a few reader-level gauging utilities could be found on computer bulletin boards (precursor to the internet). Those little beauties chewed their way through plain text or a WordStar file to produce unadorned assessment displays, some with detail added.

Among trusty DOS-based helpers I found helpful: *Fogfinder* assessed text and presented a graph that slotted the text according to popular magazines, such as Atlantic Monthly and Readers' Digest. *Wordfreq* measured word usage and presented a frequency count list. My favourite such utility, *PC-Style*, produced a graphic that reported on readability and other aspects of the text. Also handy but more elaborate, *RightWriter* and *Grammatik* measured style and grammar.

That lot worked within earlier versions of Windows, but with operating system upgrades I lost most, one by one. With Windows XP, it's a struggle to get much out of what's left of those treasured helpmates. Perhaps I could find Window-based replacements via the internet but I've yet to try. I expect that a shift to Vista would obliterate any remaining.

The meaning and use of words alter over time; for instance, *bitch* and *bastard*. In earlier years, the first referred to a female dog and the latter someone born to unmarried parents. Nowadays, among other meanings: to behave spitefully, a person regarded with contempt or resentment. The word *interesting* now suggests something more related to dull or unworthy of serious consideration, or a means to avoid saying what you really believe.

Grammar conventions also change and a writer needs to know what's acceptable and what's not, what can be used with a measure of impunity. What was unacceptable yesterday may be all right today, at least for informal writing. Also, for a particular situation or circumstance, persisting rules perhaps can be carefully bent a little. Starting a sentence with 'and' or 'but' was long a no-no; yet today both are found and accepted, as is the use of the odd no-verb sentence.

Italics or embracing quotations marks? Conventions dictate that italics are used for word emphasis, foreign words or phrases not accepted into common English usage, publication names (books, magazines), plays and movies, works of art, ships and words identified as such (...remove that second *and*...). Quotation marks, aside from dialogue, enclose direct quotes, nicknames, referenced short work (stories, poems, articles) and titles for a conference, a musical presentation or entertainment program.

Confusing? Confuses me. Why italics for a book title but bracing quotation marks for an article title? Ah well, that's why we need reference books close to hand. And, then there's punctuation as it relates to quotation marks: commas and periods within, other punctuation without. In this book I've mixed italics and quotation marks use, in particular in this section, perhaps inappropriately in some instances, but as long as a particular item properly stands out then I guess I'm not too far off the mark. Most material won't involve as many appearances of either. Consistency best, having too many quotation marks can muddy up the text (see below).

Explore other punctuation use, such as dashes and ellipses. If in doubt, punctuate, but do so sparingly. Commas are workhorses, but used to excess they can muddle rather than clarify the meaning of a phrase or sentence. Maybe it's best to start with no punctuation and then add what's absolutely needed to ensure that the text is understandable.

How punctuation is applied is controversial. Some follow the prescribed rules and others do not. Some flaunt them, ignoring even the basics required to sort out text and make it clear. I guess it's best to adopt the rules and only deviate where it appears safe to do so. For example, I do not add a comma between adjacent adjectives (replaces 'and') unless the lack of doing so obscures clarity.

Incorrect spelling or grammar quickly disconnects a publisher, may put off a reader. But many mistakes are missed and some errors are more acceptable than others, with common failings being less well received. For instance, the use of the apostrophe. *Its* and *it's*: the first is possessive (as is his, hers), the second a contraction of 'it is.' A possessive noun requires an apostrophe, as in 'the boy's dog,' although if a noun ends in an 's,' the apostrophe may follow, with or without an added 's.'

What about 'a' or 'an' before every 'h'?

The use of 'she,' 'her,' 'he,' 'him' or 'his' will cause problems for a writer who fails to check how it ties back to a character last named or otherwise identified in the text. Check pronouns used and if in doubt repeat the name or add clarifying descriptive words to avoid confusion.

Ensure that you understand basic grammar conventions. Browse a worthy helpmate (*The Canadian Style?*) or pursue the topic via the internet. Try www.ddnow.com or use a search engine (Google, Alta Vista, Yahoo?) to find other helpful sites.

Are your words solid, upright and specific? Do they engender pictures in a reader's mind, depict a setting or how a character looks or feels? Readers expect to see, hear, touch, smell or taste what's going on. Do you simply describe a setting as narrative or do you enhance it with what your characters say or do?

There are pitfalls to be avoided. For instance, some time back I was criticised for overdoing setting descriptions in my first novel, that inclination likely influenced by earlier travel writing. In following novels I curtailed that tendency, reduced the bulk, broke up the narrative description or used other means to introduce what I felt was essential.

Avoid excessive jargon, a.k.a. gobbledygook, unless intended to better define a character, say a doctor, lawyer, accountant or other professions or groups tending to lean on words best understood only by themselves (medical terms, Latin captions, debits/credits).

Don't overuse prepositions, like *of* and *with.* Tighten the sentence structure. Instead of writing '...a sky full of clouds' use '...a cloudy sky.' Instead of using '...a box with a tight lid' say '...a tightly-lidded box.' But then 'a sky full of clouds' could mean more to some than 'a cloudy sky.' Assess condensation attempts to ensure that the intended meaning isn't lost.

An adjective may be the enemy of its noun, an adverb of its verb. Cull out limp adverbs and use action/vivid/unexpected verbs. Use robust nouns rather than propping up weak ones with empty or redundant adjectives. Convert some negative verb phrasings into positive ones (The job wasn't what he wanted. -> He'd rather have another job.) and minimise the use of passive voice: *to be* derivatives (is, are, was, were).

Ever be on the lookout for overused words, those you have a tendency to repeat. I'm inclined to abuse use of the word *something*. Track down and replace such culprits. Use EDIT > FIND (mouse) or [Ctrl]+[F] (keyboard) to seek out such offenders. Also keep an eye out for backside word add-ons that detract from the quality of the word itself, such as *ize, ness, ing* or *ingly*.

Those in the know differ on what's acceptable or not, what's boring or exciting, what's to be avoided at all costs. Some don't like words ending in *ing*. Others reject word ending in *ion*. Most agree on curtailing the use of adjectives and adverbs. Accepting the basis for such dictates, I limit rather than avoid debatable words. Like clichés, there's always a place in writing where such use best addresses what's needed in the circumstances.

Favour better, more robust verbs: slugged or clipped or bludgeoned rather than hit, chatted or mumbled or droned rather than talked, trotted rather than ran, blurted out rather than said, tackled rather than worked on. If a vigorous noun evades you, then seek a vivid and descriptive adjective: a frail, stocky or deformed body; clothing that's gaudy, tasteful or flashy; auburn, shaggy or curly hair; eyes that are laughing, dreamy or twinkling; a cheerful, animated or sincere face; stern, rosebud or generous lips; a teasing, muffled or musical voice.

Contractions (it's, don't), not overdone and suitable for the context, warm up a writing style, are particularly useful in dialogue.

Without losing readers, try to expand your roster of descriptive words. Generally avoid clichés, unless they truly add value in furthering the plot, depicting a scene or a character.

Who or whom? The general rule: *who* is the subject (provides the action), *whom* the object (receives the action). But context isn't always clear, easy to sort out. I yet struggle with that pair and often settle for rewriting the passage to avoid having to decide which is correct. They receive a block of space in *Fowler's Modern English Usage* but, after working my way through that explanation, I found myself little the wiser.

On the other hand, via www.odnow.com (other items explained) Grammar Girl offered a measure of clarity, and an example: 'Whom do I love?' If the response could be 'I love him.' (target of love) then *whom* is correct—m and m ending! For me, reversing the question and response works better: He (subject) was involved. -> Who was involved? She (subject) trusted him (object). -> Whom did she trust? Well, maybe...

Watch for inconsistencies and contradictions: numbers or words appearing in two places that should be the expressed the same way (3 or three, grey or gray,).

Keep an eye out for redundancy, unintended repetition of words.

While both *criticize* and *criticise* are correct, try to avoid mixing 's' and 'z' in the same word where it's appears more than once within the material.

Keep an eye out for *me* versus *I* errors relative to preposition and pronoun phrases. '...with John and *me*.' –> correct; '...with John and *I*.' –> incorrect. On the other hand, test a sentence ending to see if a verb, purposely left out, can be added: He can sing better than I (*can* omitted). If so, *I* is correct and *me* is not—despite the fact that in conversation *me* is more likely to be heard in such phrases.

Weed out exclamation marks. Few should be used and then only for particular emphasis or an exclamation, a voice raised in anger or protest.

Make use of transitional words to indicate a shift or change from a previous sentence or paragraph. Direction: above, nearby, below. Contrast: however, nevertheless, but, still, yet. Compare: likewise, similarly. Summary: hence, on the whole, in brief. Time passage: until, meanwhile, later, afterwards. To add or emphasise: besides, furthermore, lastly.

To effectively exploit words, those that best enhance the material must be combined properly. If a novice writer eager to learn, carefully consider a general writing class, course or workshop. But, they're not all equal. Like anything else, some are good and others not. Scan the outline and if possible talk to the presenter. A general course considered or attended, then seek focused courses (dialogue, revision) to enhance your writing skills.

Most writers develop a hangup or two, habits that may well irritate others. I shorten the likes of 'sorted out' and 'couple of' to 'sorted' (as Brits do) and 'couple.' Also, I try to curtail the use of 'need be,' accepting that some form of 'needed' or 'should be' would be more acceptable.

Despite the battle being lost with good/well, fewer/less and number/amount. For the latter two: can count items and cannot. A dwindling number of writers desperately hang onto what's yet grammatically correct. And to be avoided at all cost is anything at all comparable to what so degrades the spoken word: 'right, like, you know, I mean and uhm...'
Other words often confused or used improperly, a sampling:

- are or is: two nouns with 'and' between -> are, with 'or' between -> is
(The cat and dog are... The dog or cat is...)
- can or may: being able to, being permitted to
(I can do it. May I go now?)
- no one or no-one: the latter is more a British usage and what I use
- farther or further: distance versus moving forward or in addition
(Toronto is farther away than Winnipeg. The situation was further explored.)
- good or well: an adjective, usually an adverb
(He ran a good race. How well she's doing.)
- imply or infer: to suggest, to draw a conclusion
(You imply, suggest. I infer, deduce.)
- its or it's: possessive pronoun, a contraction of 'it is'
(The dog scratched its back. It's a long way to go.)

- principal (as an adjective) or principle: a major position, a fundamental truth or rule (a noun) (That was his principal objection. There are principles to consider.)
- like or as: use comparatively, inferior substitute for *while* or *when*
- lay or lie: to place, to recline
- oral or verbal: word of mouth, spoken or written

Affect or effect? To sort out this thorny pair, I consulted *Fowler's Modern English Usage* and *A Writer's Handbook of Current English* and then turned to a friend for his perspective. From Fowler's...(pg 13): These verbs are not synonyms...words of totally different meanings... Affect: have an influence on, effect a change in, concern. Effect: bring about, cause, secure. This could affect his recovery (influence). This could effect his recovery (cause). This does not affect me (concern). This will not effect his purpose (secure). From A Writer's Handbook...(pg 519): Affect is a verb meaning 'influence' - effect is a noun meaning 'result.' The weather affected our tempers. The frightened child affected a defiant look. The effects of radiation are not yet completely known. Affect is also a noun...and effect is a formal verb... Added by me: His efforts affected the results (influenced). His efforts effected the results (caused). His effect on the jury was remarkable. According to a couple dictionaries consulted, affect as a noun has become largely obsolete.

That or which? This pair warrants extensive coverage in *Fowler's Modern English Usage*, that representing a measure of the decision challenge. Compare that to what some pundits promote: ...avoid *which* if at all possible. *That* is usually the correct one to use, *which* being more often used in a restricted sense. And, after reading a sentence using *that*, you may find that even that can be deleted without harming the sentence.

Got all that in hand, having done a bit of added digging into a tome or two? Now string all those spiffy words together, appropriately. Vary sentence length. Short sentences pick up the pace and more lengthy ones tend to slow things down. Generally shorter paragraphs are better, although varying paragraph size usually improves most written material. Articles destined for a newspaper or magazine lean toward shorter sentences and paragraphs, with one sentence often a paragraph.

Proportional blank space on a page appeals to a reader's eye more than viewing a page jammed with text and bordered by meagre margins.

To gain an appreciation of words and how to use them, you may wish to consider joining a writing group, what could be considered a writing course of sorts. Such gatherings are a great place to acquire writing experience. Hear what others have assembled. Read your creation. Compare notes. Share critiquing. Receive alternate word choices. Obtain feedback on how others perceive your work.

A past member of PWAC (Periodical Writers...), CAA (Canadian Authors...) and, more locally, VWS (Victoria Writers...)—all helpful associations—as a senior I joined two Victoria-area writing groups and find both helpful, with social aspects a bonus.

What is the point of having a good grasp of words and how to string them together without a comfortable and productive means of committing them to paper? Writers differ and each needs to find her or his particular approach to that task, a method that fits within an already established lifestyle.

For some a regimented schedule or routine works best. For others, inspiration and enthusiasm play bigger roles. What do you think or expect will work best for you? Two or three hours a day, rain or shine? Fewer days at the computer keyboard but longer sessions?

The choice matters less than how successful the routine becomes, how it works for you. Production and quality are the measures. Trash in, trash out? Getting the job done, generating quality material will determine what works best.

Not having a deadline to meet and being retired, I don't have a fixed routine as such. Early morning is my productive time of day, no matter what gets produced: writing or other computer-related chores such as computer protection updating, banking and email exchanges.

My computer is usually on four or so days a week and, aside from email and other internet chores, the current writing project receives first attention, the benefit of a four-five o'clock or so start, a fresher enthusiasm. In between computer sessions I read or attack pages like these with a red pen.

Based upon results, I've found that pushing myself, trying to force myself to write, dries up any productive or inspirational juices left in me at my age.

What do you think a successful routine might be for you? Try different approaches until you find one that improves your quality output or productivity.

Short Stories +

Some writers never abandon a desire to write a book, be it fiction or non-fiction. Others are content to create short stories, essays or articles. Many scribes never attempt to get their work published. Perhaps they don' t consider it good enough, or they just can't be bothered doing all that's needed to produce and find a home for their efforts: proper structuring, addressing a required or suitable word count, deciding where to send the piece, follow-up and persistence. They're content to commit their thoughts to paper and perhaps send it along to family or friends, maybe read it within a writing group.

If you expect or hope to write a book at some point, investing some initial time and energy in writing a short story or two could provide a great training ground. Completing a book demands a considerably more substantial commitment than creating articles or short stories. Starting small would give you a chance to progressively learn about writing, get a feel for promoting yourself and what you've achieved.

How do recognised writers come up with all that good stuff? Just like you can: family incidents, personal experiences, places visited, memories of people known and lost or left behind, comments overheard, observations while out and about, perhaps a vivid dream. Or maybe they happen upon an item in a newspaper or magazine, or see or hear something on television or radio.

Each and every day presents writing prompts and possibilities, material just waiting to be explored or exploited, committed to paper. That's why many dedicated writers always carry a pen and notepad—no serious writer wants to come up with a good idea and then lose it to a memory lapse.

Writing for children and young adults requires that the tale unfold from the perspective of someone of a similar age. Like poetry and some aspects of humour, it's a niche market, one that's very competitive. To get a better idea of what works and not, browse the shelves of libraries and bookshops, do some online searching. Note the mix of pictures and limited text for the much younger set. Recall your early years and readings for children that you attended. Which stories grabbed your attention and that of those around you: content or how it was delivered?

Newspapers or magazines can be a tough market to crack. To get a better idea of what's needed and/or wanted, browse copies of possible publications (in a library?) with your project in mind. Ask yourself what a targeted recipient appears to want, and if that is something you can provide? Are browsed articles long or short? How are they structured? What tense is used most? Is material personalised or not? Newspapers and magazines lean toward shorter paragraphs than books.

To be successful you need an edge, something that sets your work apart from what a like-minded mob hopes will succeed, will reach the desk of someone receptive. One and all are ever trying to get a leg up over the competition. Starting out, community papers or regional magazines are easier to access than publications with a wider readership.

Persistent pursuit and consistent submissions can pay off in other ways. I ended up with a seniors' newspaper column as a result of sending (and resending) a query and writing sample to a publication that proved to be one segment of a larger newsprint organisation.

One reason I shelved articles and switched to books some years ago was a growing dissatisfaction with having to deal with editors/publishers. While they do have the right to make changes, some can become awkward, particularly if they try to make content changes that distort a writer's intentions for an article.

I encountered such an incident, one that involved computer material. The changes made reflected badly on me, made me appear as if I didn't know what I was writing about. My complaint was rejected, and I did continue to write for that publication, for a while.

Editors do call the shots and somewhat control the purse strings. If you are faced with a similar situation, confront such folk with caution; the cost may exceed the value of the objection.

Travel writing has long been a market worth pursuing. There are many publications eager to get their

hands on well-written material (+ pictures) for destinations of interest to readers. An added benefit of
profitable writing of this sort is that you may get to
write off against taxable income a portion of the
applicable travel costs.

To get some idea of writing style, browse articles
in targeted publications. Also note the picture quality—can you produce something equivalent? How are
the pieces assembled: chronologically or otherwise?
And do remember that smaller publications are often
easier to access.

If organising a trip you expect to write about, plan
ahead. While a digital camera is best, if you have a
scanner (or access to one), take along a disposable
camera or two. Few of those are stolen. Duplicate
important shots, just in case.

Pack a few pads and pens and keep notes during
the trip. Having previously researched the destination, after arrival gather material or books locally
available. Books I've bought on trips I've never encountered at home.

Digital cameras offer writers notable advantage.
Submitting pictures electronically as email attachments sure beats having to mail photos, perhaps
never to see them again.

For older camera film shots or sketches, a scanner (all-in-one printer?) produces a digital picture
file. JPEG is a common format and a TIFF format
may provide a sharper image. Photoshop Elements
(an older version may accompany a digital camera)
converts some picture-file formats.

An article in hand, seek publication guidelines
and clarify any unclear requirements. Scrutinise
submission strictures, such as how to send your

piece (likely by electronic means): within email or as an attachment? Note any required word count.

Send your item along and don't forget to include mention of any expertise or track record that favours the submission. If you get lucky, have a submission accepted, be prepared to have your piece edited for content and for fit within the publication.

Network with other writers of your genre, share experiences and discoveries. Someone I know got in touch with a crime writers organisation and received unexpected assistance that was truly impressive.

Enter contests related to your interests.

Find out who knows whom, who has a connected relative or friend.

Success seldom comes to those who sit back and wait for something to drift their way.

Back in the 1980s I started writing for computer publications and enjoyed a measure of success before moving on to include travel material. After all but abandoning article writing I started working on a first novel. My best ever writing earnings resulted from contributing computer sections for an accounting text.

Moving west in 1996 I contributed newsletter items for a computer club I belonged to and then tackled a few western-based publications.

Nowadays I work on books and articles targeting seniors, an age grouping I now share.

Is there a niche market that appeals to you, represents something you can address with understanding?

Later sections on creating a manuscript cover a range of writing considerations. While you may not be interested in tackling a book, do read those sections and the one on organising a book, in search of items equally applicable to short stories and articles. Such as: show, don't tell. And bringing into play as many of a reader's five senses as possible: smell, taste, hearing, seeing and feeling.

Remember, if you want others to appreciate your efforts, what you write must truly matter to you. And it should be something you understand. Incidents or characters with which you are familiar are always easier to write about.

Do you have a writing framework in mind? Are you writing for yourself, for family or do you really want to get that tale or essay out into the vast world of commercially printed material?

Assuming the latter, your creation isn't finished just because it's committed to paper. Have you satisfied all the essentials, such as a satisfactory opening, captivating content and a tidy finish? Where is the finished product now to go? How will that be achieved? A clear plan of action is essential, as are determination and persistence.

Perhaps one way to launch the submission routine, gain a bit of experience, is to try a letter or email to the editor, taking exception to an item discovered in the newspaper or on television. Unless such a submission is exceptional, shorter items have a better chance of getting printed than longer ones.

That exposure in hand, check libraries, newspapers and the internet for short story submission opportunities, or try a postcard contest, where the word count cannot exceed some two hundred and fifty or so—now there's a writing challenge!

Writing contests can be both enjoyable and frustrating. If later made available, you may not wish to read the winning submissions. While you may or may not admire your own work, you'll likely find the winners lacking in some respect, judge that they are no better than what you sent in, perhaps even less deserving. Nonetheless, entering such competitions can only contribute to improving writing skills. In submitting material be sure that you meet all the rules and requirements, pay any required fee.

What about multiple market opportunities? Recognise which rights are attached to an article payment. If locally placed, sold, without restrictions, flog the perhaps-altered (content changed or adapted in part, shortened or lengthened?) piece to distant towns, other provinces or countries. Why waste all that effort?

I expect that most writers today use a computer. Keyboards, monitors and boxes with flashing lights have made writing easier in so many ways: built-in spell checking, ready access to wads of internet information, easier revisions (deleting or inserting text, shifting sentences or paragraphs), programs that will assess material. And, when it comes time to submit the end product, unless specified otherwise, snail-mail is usually the last option.

The days of sending in a neatly typed double-spaced pages with wide margins are largely history, even for manuscripts. Newspapers and magazines don't have the time to key in what arrives on paper. Nor do they wish to scan in material and then attempt to fix what doesn't accommodate OCR (optical character recognition) standards. They want text electronically, single-spaced and using a fairly common font such as Times-Roman, sized ten-point or larger. Sans serif fonts may work for headings in a book but oddball typefaces are best restricted to personal use. Check submission guidelines and follow each and every one of them—that is if you want to improve the possibility of acceptance.

Although more people use email than fax, from time to time I've found the latter facility helpful. An email address may not be provided but a fax number may appear. My computer has a fax modem card, as did earlier gear. A dial-up internet connection is slower but works for me. I've sent lots of faxes but have received only one or two. I don't include a cover sheet on faxes sent but do include header data on faxes sent (receiver identification and subject; my name, address, date and email address).

For those using a high-speed access service or lacking a fax modem, fax facilities can be found on the internet (at a cost).

Electronic communications benefit both sender and receiver. Think about it. As a sender, no postage to pay or self-addressed return envelope for material that might be returned. Evolution hasn't always produced positive results but marrying writing and electronics has worked well, has become a godsend. I send material for a newspaper column by email, with any picture files attached.

Some publications may accept or wish to receive material as a wordprocessor document (retains formatting), with any applicable pictures also attached to the covering email message. Others may prefer article content submitted as email text.

One of two writing groups I belong to produces an annual anthology that bundles member contributions, provides a means for some members to see their work in print. For anthologies I've adapted book chapters and articles, those pending query or already printed elsewhere.

Never having won any attempted, I nowadays ignore writing contests and squander the nominal fees elsewhere.

A great source of available and handy material is to become your own clipping service. Years ago I started extracting items from magazines and newspapers and tucking the material away for possible future use. I even got to use some of it. While it's an excellent idea, the speed with which files become fat can become frightening, even burdensome if you have to shift the material at some point.

And don't forget that notepad and pen. You never know when something might pop up. Hoping that a thought or sight will come back to you later isn't good enough. Even at a younger age the mind cannot be depended upon.

A Short Story

What is a short story? How is it constructed? What content is essential? Worthy questions, important considerations.

Unlike with a book, where ample space is available to deal with necessary components, a short story requires a writer to condense the tale, disclose setting and characters within limited space, while ensuring that a reader understands and appreciates what is transpiring.

And, how best can that be managed? Lengthy descriptions won't fit but pointed suggestions might. Is there a word that will do the job of many, perhaps something displayed by dialogue (idiom?) or a defining activity?

That means that within a pre-determined size or permitted word count you must adequately condense an incident without losing anything of substance, introduce and resolve in an enticing way what it is that you wish to say.

To produce a piece of good writing you need some kind of unique story slant or a distinctive means of delivery. Is your tale one waiting to be told? Does it excite you? If not, then why should it excite a reader? Would the prospect of writing about the topic entice you away from delving into another chapter or two of that book by a favoured author?

A short story or an article has narrow boundaries. Its theme or focus must be clear and it needs a catchy opening and a satisfying closing. The time span within the tale is usually short: an hour or two, a day, a week?

Characters should be limited to one or two, perhaps three if handled well. Ensure that each and every character contributes. While there's more room for dialogue in a book, there might well be a place within the tale where carefully structured conversation works best.

As for essentials, a short story may lack the space available in a book but it must accomplish the same goal. How much can be accomplished within the space permitted? A first draft may well exceed limitations, and that's where editing enters the process.

Without harming the content, revise and trim the material until the target fit is achieved. Disclose the essentials by character action or speech rather than dull narrative.

What detail must be included? What can safely be left out? Every word used must count, must enhance what's going on. There's no room for unneeded adjectives or adverbs, excessive descriptions, boring add-ins or anything else that doesn't truly contribute and carry the tale forward.

Be brutal! Cut and rephrase and then do it again. All done, get someone to read what you've achieved, asking that (s)he be totally objective, even unkind if need be, in assessing the material.

Wow, finally you're done! Really? Not so. Set the piece aside and have another go at it later, before sending it anywhere.

Read it aloud, attempting to do so as if someone else had written it. Does it sound as good as it did earlier? Better? Or, are there parts that now don't measure up? Rewrite, a major component of writing, is what any good writer performs over and over again. In my case, what I produce is likely 30% creation and 70% revision.

To repeat, even if writing a book isn't what you want or intend to tackle, do browse the sections on organising a book and preparing a manuscript for details equally applicable to short stories or articles.

An Essay

And what is an essay? Definitions may vary but the core intent doesn't. An essay is a short non-fiction composition wherein a writer expresses an idea, puts forth an opinion or debates an issue, in the hope that the material will entertain a reader or perhaps convert her or him to the writer's particular view-point or opinion. In an organised fashion the content will explain, analyze or evaluate a topic. A newspaper editorial is one form of an essay.

An essay should display originality of approach and substance. To be a winner it must add to a readers understanding of a particular topic. An essay should avoid the ornate or complicated in favour of simplicity and clarity. Curtail preamble, get into the substance and provide the meat of the topic. An activity. An event or person. A valued item or principle. A trip or unusual experience.

Topic in hand, ensure that you know whereof you speak. Research for an essay is mandatory, is needed to assemble all the pertinent facts needed to back up the premise. Research the targeted item in libraries (ask the librarian?) and via the internet.

Facts in hand, expound away, but with care and staying on topic. Be logical and reinforce the core theme. Pay attention to detail and presentation. Don't wander off into anything unrelated.

As to the writing itself, the same rules used for other forms of presentation apply. All done, read it aloud and then rewrite. Read it again and revise some more. The resulting material must be both accurate and engaging.

All in order, a bit of polishing never goes amiss. Substitute active voice for passive. Use 'He decided.' rather than 'It was decided by him.' 'Achieving perfection requires added effort.' rather than 'Added effort is required to achieve perfection.'

Humour

Wonderful short stories, articles and essays, adorned with bone-tickling humour, have been written through the years. Few incidents are truly funny in themselves. How the situation is handled or described creates the humour. What have you read recently that made you chuckle? Were sentences short and punchy? What in particular tickled your fancy? Can you adapt what you discovered to your writing? A bit of applicable humour seldom goes amiss.

Publishers and editors are ever on the lookout for good humour. Being able to make readers smile, chuckle or laugh is a talent, one shared by few writers. It's not a skill I possess and it appears to be something not easy to teach, except by example. Is it a capability one either possesses or does not?

Readers differ as to what they find funny, but keeping it simple seems best, whether for narrative or dialogue.

Is there a type of humour that would work for you? Something unexpected occurring. Misinterpretation. Innuendo. A stock joke introduced. Something self-deprecating. Should you try to write humour, ask yourself if what you have in mind, what you find funny, will amuse other folk. Try it out on family or friends. Did they laugh? No? Back to the drawing board...

Offer a reader something unanticipated. Set aside logic and personal dignity concepts. Simplicity usually beats complexity. Writing humour has been compared to writing poetry: meter and rhythm, beats and pacing, structure and timing. How about introducing a reader-gripping hook, a reader-stopping punch line or a twisty ending?

And, what's off limits? Not much it appears, but there are a few taboos: anything disgusting or repulsive, words offensive to feelings or prevailing and accepted societal norms, excessive profanity, being overly crude or vulgar? Ethnic humour should be used with added care; it can be hurtful. Avoid sarcasm. Don't insult or put anyone down—yourself aside perhaps.

Ignore the taboos and proceed at your peril; be prepared to have what you've spent so long compiling and polishing fall flat on its whatever. While standards do alter, they do so in an evolving fashion. What was unacceptable yesterday may be more welcomed tomorrow, but not necessarily today.

Tricky names, expressions or character quirks might work. Try rephrasing descriptions in more vivid ways. Find a way to introduce a surprise, frustration or some kind of quirky conflict.

As mentioned, I'm not inclined to be a funny guy and I've yet to discover how to effectively change that for writing purposes. But I do at times try and have achieved limited success. Thus far, I've found taking an occasional shot at myself seems to work.

Helpmates abound for many aspects of writing but I've unearthed few books that deal with humour, aside from examples from humorists that might yield some clues. At two writing groups I belong to, only a few members have displayed that talent. They share delightful tidbits that please one and all and raise envy from those of us lacking the ability.

Finding little of interest on bookshelves aside from offerings written by humorists, I turned to cyberspace and found a few humour-related items. But the web content is ever changing and whatever is in short supply today may become more abundant tomorrow.

Surprisingly, some of what I found appears to be little more than a tweaking of words and phrases otherwise used in writing not intended to titillate. Shorter sentences. An anecdote. Surprise. Offbeat nouns or verbs. Something ridiculous yet believable. Oddball character names. Peculiar imagery. Odd twists. Pomposity deflated. Weird frustration. Provocative comparisons. A ridiculous name for a common item. A what-if situation to tickle the fancy.

Perhaps it's best to seek supposedly funny books (peruse before purchasing) that relate to your intentions. For instance, for an upcoming non-fiction book about twelve years on a Malahat farm, I scoured shelves and the web for humour that related to animals or farming...with little success.

Through the years we've been exposed to some firstrate comics, in writing, on the stage and on television. Consider how those gals or guys tickled your funny bone, made you laugh. What was it? Delivery. Choice of words. How important was the visual? Jack Benny was a master of his craft; who better used silence and a stare. In nearer times, the *Air Farce* and *Twenty-Two Minutes* deliver some great sketches and one-liners. But how much of that stuff would work on paper, for you?

If you encounter a funny incident make a note of what you found appealing and consider how you think it might be adapted or tweaked to suit your efforts. What has happened in your life that made you laugh? When last did others laugh at what you said or did, and if so, why?

Satire. According to one dictionary: '...it's a literary work in which vices, follies, stupidities, abuses and such are held up to ridicule and contempt.' – and- 'the use of ridicule, sarcasm, irony and such to expose, attack or deride vices, follies, etc.' Irony, the use of word to express an opposite meaning, can also add humour. While I accept that satire and irony may be found funny, I doubt I'll put either to use. It's not my bag, as some say. To each her or his own, I guess...

The best way to get a handle on humour writing is to read what the masters of the craft have produced. Much of it has passed the test of time and is still funny. Like P.G. Wodehouse. Check the humour section of bookshelves at a library or larger bookstore. Or, haunt used book disposals or garage sales, where you might find great stuff at bargain prices.

You mustn't tell a reader that an item is funny. A reader must discover that on her or his own. Appeal to a reader's sense of sight or smell or taste or feel or sound. Create snappy dialogue or an offbeat description of a situation.

Similes and metaphors may prove helpful. Well-structured dialogue might work. Adding a dollop of humour to a manuscript can only enhance the final product, assuming that it meshes with what you are writing about.

And Then What?

When I first wrote an article that was accepted and printed I was elated, to say the least. But after managing to get considerably more material published I ran into difficulties with a few editors. I had no problem with them changing words (that's their prerogative), but I objected to having the sense of material altered. I stopped submitting material and attempted to write a book—an undertaking totally different.

But a couple books in hand, I found staying away difficult and I returned to writing articles, choosing to pursue a narrower range of destinations, to latterly focus on seniors as a target audience.

Today's marketplace for writers is competitive. Whether writing a short story, an article or a manuscript you'll need to identify and gather suitable material, unearth ideas that are unusual or unique.

I use a bulletin board to store ideas that pop up, items worth saving for a later quick browse in search of anything that might fit an article just getting underway. Would that work for you or is there something else that would better serve the purpose?

What is the focus or theme to be? What will best grab the attention of a reader? To open with the best material or tweak a reader's interest with something colourful or teasing and then launch into the gist of the theme. To work your way into what you want to say. Or, to leave the best stuff for later in the piece, when something peppier may be needed.

The internet is a godsend to those seeking data: lots and lots of material for the asking, perhaps too much at times. Searches need to be narrowed (+, -, enclosing a phrase in quotation marks) to isolate the good stuff for extraction (highlight and copy to the clipboard, paste into a Notepad file?).

Be aware of libel, making defamatory remarks, intruding upon or offending someone's reputation. If in doubt, don't. Exclude whatever it was that you had planned to include.

Common knowledge aside, a failure to divulge the source of words and ideas found in the writing of others may amount to plagiarism, depending upon the extent of adoption. Ethics demand that source material heavily utilised be acknowledged. For sure, direct quotes or lifting out sections of what someone else has written and dropping it into your work without providing credit is a definite no-no.

But there's an enormous grey area. Words and ideas arise and evolve over years and it's often impossible to determine ownership or an original source. Clichés for example—who dreamed those up? Anyway, it's best to be aware of the matter and ensure that it doesn't enter your work.

Selling Material

Be prepared for rejection, or more likely being ignored. Not pleasant, it's common when submitting short stories, articles or books. Over time it becomes less irritating. Try not to take it personally; it's not intended as such.

Through the years, aside from receiving no response at all, I've accumulated a pile of dismissive messages, those mostly from earlier years when getting a response was more likely.

To lessen the pain, try not to get your hopes up. Keep busy. Tackle other projects. Assume that getting any kind of reply will take time. If you get a negative response, note any accompanying comments. The best of writers have been rejected at some time or other. Read the 'flogging' section for more on this.

To ease the pursuit, choose a niche market: young children, teenagers, seniors, travel, business. From the internet or a library, create a list of potential contacts and email addresses. Send out a carefully crafted query. Keep track of any responses. As appropriate, follow those up politely and don't give up easily.

In preparation, create a means to keep track of when and to where (to whom?) material was sent. Be careful not to duplicate material sent out for particular consideration within a common publication area. Unless an article sale includes some kind of a restriction, precludes other use of the material, do send it out to other marketing or publication areas, perhaps modified to accommodate the new destination.

To keep track of articles I send out I use a columnar listing that records target identification details and what was sent and when. I used to request tear sheets for what got published and even got a few. On occasion I received a copy of the applicable publication. Initially, I noted which items were accepted and tracked payment. After a period of satisfactory dealings with any one publication, I accepted that I'd be paid.

If or when you catch the attention of an editor, and establish a working relationship, take care to maintain it. For instance, if another more lucrative contact comes along that conflicts with the first one, in the same market area, give some thought to which should be given first consideration—the oldest, the one that pays the best or the one that has printed more of your articles? Publications come and go and you don't know which one over the long haul will outlive the other.

An Article Example

What follows is an article about digital cameras printed in a 2006 seniors column. As others submitted for the column, it contained some six hundred words, a count often adjusted, not by me, to accommodate available newspaper space. What's good about it? And not? Does the opening capture attention and encourage a reader to read on? Does the closing wrap things up properly? Does the content adequately cover the subject? Anything missing?

Last year we replaced our camera. After providing good service over many years, rather than rewinding automatically at picture twenty-four, the camera started doing that after the fourth picture was taken. Considering the likely repair cost, we decided to enter the twenty-first century, purchase a digital model and upgrade the computer to handle camera picture files.

Upgrading the somewhat long in the tooth computer considered debatable, I bought a new one that included provision for handling the digital memory sticks or cards inserted into a camera for storing the photos taken. Pictures transferred to the computer could then be sent to friends and family or be printed. A picture resizer available on Microsoft's website will reduce a 1.5 megabyte photo file to 100-200 kilobytes or so, a better size for sending view-only pictures as email attachments for people like me who are still using a slower dialup internet connection.

Given comparable functions, operating a digital camera differs little from a film model. But the newer technology permits, among other things, viewing what's been taken or is about to be taken, on a camera screen (1.5" and larger). Using the viewer, however, shortens battery life. It's best to carry along an extra battery that's been topped up if a rechargeable.

A memory stick only holds so many pictures and dealing with discards on the computer rather than using the camera viewer for deletion decisions will extend camera battery life. But, if you're out and about and the stick in the camera and a spare are both filled, by all means delete a lesser picture to make room for that shot that cannot be missed.

The camera's picture mega-pixel (dots that make up a photo) count can be adjusted. The higher the number, the sharper the photo, and the fewer the pictures that can be stored on a memory stick. Sticks come in capacities that range from 16MB (mega/million bytes) on up to 512+MB. While a 16MB (may come with camera) is suitable as a backup for the one in a camera, nothing less than a 64MB is really worth buying. We found that a couple 64MB memory sticks best suits our routine: after printing pictures the stick is erased and later exchanged for a filled one removed from the camera.

For an added investment in a photo-quality printer and special paper, excellent pictures can be printed at home. Optionally, pictures can be printed commercially from the memory stick or, as we chose to handle the task, by copying them to a rewritable CD and processing from that. The cost per print is now less than twenty cents and customer-friendly photo-processing machines permit cropping, sizing, brightness adjustment and requesting extra copies. Programs like Photoshop accommodate more extensive picture manipulation.

If you own a scanner or have access to one, non-digital pictures can be converted to digital photo files. The file quality selected, if adjustable, should address the intended use for the picture: lesser for view-only email attachments, a larger file for printing to achieve a crisper image.

Flexibility recommends digital photography for the average consumer. Well, aside from this wrinkly luddite. I've avoided cameras for years, ever since I realized that cameras and I don't get along. I have a box of pictures taken from some neat spots around the world. In half the photos I can't identify the location. In others the object of the shot is too distant to make the photo worth keeping.

On one trip I took along an instant camera. Now, years later, those deteriorating pictures are all but useless. On a trip to Japan that included Hong Kong, I purchased an inexpensive camera that came with instructions in Japanese. Fortunately pretty much point and click, it worked well for years, until the flash unit expired.

These days my wife takes the pictures, I deal with the computer segment and she handles the CD developing routine.

Organising
A Book

Putting together a book, combining all the bits and pieces into a finished product, could be compared to assembling and decorating a model. Words the pieces, structure and style represent the glue and paint. But differing with writing, after assembly and a measure of embellishment, you're not done; work remains.

What's been written must be scrutinised and then again, expanded or reduced, taken apart and re-arranged with sentences or paragraphs shifted about, within one section or to another. And, that's before final tidy-up and polishing, and all else that must be done thereafter, such as conversion for printing, later marketing and follow-up. And, truth-fully, a book is never really finished. Rewriting should only stop when you feel totally drained or, a massive effort invested, you can no longer stand the sight of the manuscript. And that's more than likely to happen.

Several decades ago, as a result of discussions with an acquaintance, I agreed to contribute an accounting text that was destined to become part of a set that would embrace differing business disciplines. Despite having the business familiarity, at the time I was a tad shy of writing experience and how to approach that project. Nonetheless, I was one of few who actually completed a rough manuscript. As disorganised as my contribution was at that point, I was unprepared to invest extra time on it unless assured that the project was headed for completion. A good decision as it turned out. With few others fulfilling their commitment, the entire project fizzled and died. What did I learn from the experience? There's considerably more to writing than just putting words on pages.

Today's writing marketplace is fiercely competitive and for a manuscript to capture that all-important reader attention, it must be meaningful and contain material and ideas judged by others as being worthwhile, outstanding or unusual. And, obviously, it must be well written.

While perhaps appearing an awkward, more expensive, way to going about it, in putting together a book, consider selling a few copies of a completed product and then sending a query or copy to a targeted publisher (or two) for consideration—along with a few favourable reader responses and proposed alteration notes. That may prove a better bet than trying to find a home for the original manuscript/typescript. With all the competition out there, seeking a different way to capture the attention of a publisher cannot be overlooked.

Organising and writing what's between the covers of a book requires attention and care—lots of it. And persistence. Don't give up. Keep at it, despite despair and debating why you bother or how much you really care at the moment. Relax. Take a break. Being all tied up in knots smothers creativity. For most of us, anxiety won't go away; it'll ever hover, to appear and reappear along the way, no matter what.

To get a better idea of all that's needed for your book, browse library and bookshop shelves; scan the interior of books that catch your attention. See how others have assembled the assorted components to enhance their books.

Stories, whether a short tale or a book, gather scenes together, introduce dramatic episodes (perhaps condensing what transpires) and include dialogue to add immediacy. A scene could be one in an ongoing flow of events or a flashback to introduce character or storyline background information, with transitional words added to smooth timeframe shifts.

Is your intended storyline strong? Unique? New plots are scarce. Most tales are variations on those reworked through the years, altered by different characters or a shift in locale. Old plots, new twists. Find ways to distinguish what you write from what others offer. Strive to make it better. Check the pacing of your work. Is it monotonous or sluggish, carelessly crafted or slapdash?

Content representing bones, assembly, structure and presentation are the skeleton and skin, what's needed to bring or hold it all together. A well-conceived cover provides the ensemble, what in days long gone by would have been fashionable for males upward mobile, in the form of dress for a well-turned-out dandy.

A book's exterior is without doubt what first catches the attention of a potential reader. The wrapping first helps to sell the product: cover, spine and what appears on the back (see section on the cover). Creating the enclosing packaging may involve someone else, but what's inside is the author's domain, her or his ultimate responsibility.

Book content varies according to its nature but each book contains a title page with publication information on its back. A first page inside the front cover of a novel may provide a story synopsis, an excerpt from the tale or book review comment. A disclaimer and dedication may be included, along with a prologue and/or epilogue.

A non-fiction book could include a contents listing and introduction, attributes for research data, supporting artwork or graphics.

Unless the information (plus a picture?) appears on the inside of the back cover, a last page often outlines the author's background, achievements or other interests.

In addition to a book's wrapping, intended to encourage delving further, how you open your tale is crucial. You need a hook, a means to grab attention and introduce something that can be ratcheted upward with added intensity and cooled down, with eventual resolution. Time and place established, why not introduce a sub-plot or deviation to add character dimension.

Will a prologue or preamble add value: something to set up the tale or an extracted snippet of the tale and placed upfront? If so, rather than trying to say what it is, consider using a symbol instead. That's what I did in my third novel, using the same one in this book.

Is your prologue or, that lacking, the first chapter strong, the first sentence a grabber? Does conflict appear in early pages? A book opening must encourage a reader to dig deeper and explore what's to be found in following pages.

Is an epilogue required to tie up loose ends, or to bridge the book to another to follow? Most readers are happiest when, completing a book, there are no overlooked significant dangling story details, unresolved issues or incidents. End your tale properly. Don't leave a reader frustrated. Sad may be acceptable if it suits the storyline, but a happier frame of mind is usually better.

Readers want to be part of what unfolds, vicariously, without bearing any personal responsibility or having to actually endure what ensues, any aftermath.

Will your story include tried and true components: incidents, excitement, emotion, complications and suspense, crisis and climax, resolution? That's what readers want; all that plus engaging dialogue. That's what keeps readers involved and turning pages, pursuing answers to wrinkles in the plot that pop up.

Conflict involves a reader. How about a dollop of frustration? A hint of what's to come? Appeal to potential reader phobias. Add a cliff-hanger, some sort of surprise. Let nature's fury add flavour. Ignore the essentials and your tale will whither and the reader will cast the book aside and seek another.

Writing style is important. Think about books recently sampled by you and then tossed aside. Why the rejection? Was the writing sloppy or choppy, hard to follow or just plain dull? Try to achieve a comfortable writing style, one that will also appeal to potential book buyers. As for the words you commit to paper, seek an independent opinion and heed any response, paying extra attention to negative comment.

Is suspense to be included? Most tales are enhanced by something left out, perhaps hinted at, something kept just out of reach, sight or hearing; a situation suggested to the reader but as yet unknown to the characters involved. However used, suspense introduced must be believable and relate to reality.

If intending to employ an issue, situation or anything at all in doubt, invest the necessary time to check it out. Know whereof you speak. For example, while not essential to what unfolds, my protagonist in three novels was an accountant, a vocation with which I'm familiar. Related aspects of what he did and how he did it hopefully added flavouring to the tales.

You want readers to feel that they are getting their money's worth, to stay with you, not quit and move on to another book. Introduce a problem or trouble, perfection gone awry or a description that surpasses expectations. An intriguing letter. Something debatable or outrageous. And don't forget that all-important gripping dialogue.

Will your chapter content measure up? Are setting descriptions as they should be, not too brief or excessive? Are characters properly fleshed out and interesting, some appealing and others off-putting?

Do timeframes (past, present, future) and shifts between in the story make sense?

Do all chapters get somewhere? How should you close out a scene or chapter? Just let it dribble or fizzle away? Wrongo! That's a reader loser. Au contraire. You need to offer something that'll make it hard for a reader to set the book aside, even briefly. A turn of events that conjures up images of what may yet appear. A secret partially disclosed. A question left unanswered. A critical mistake almost made. A disturbing comment dropped.

Planning to burden readers with bulky narrative? Not on! Spread it about in manageable chunks, interspersed with carefully crafted dialogue.

Suggest what's in play, what will unfold. Involve the reader. Make her or him imagine some of what's needed to flesh out a scene or character. That breeds interest.

In addition to being addicted to writing and the use of words, a writer must be her or his own worst, most severe, critic. Don't leave that chore solely to others. Improvement results from how a writer reacts to what's already committed to paper (or screen). Does it flow nicely or is it choppy? Is something missing or is what's written notably deficient? If so, to what degree and where?

Avoid the adequate. Reach higher. Scrutinize books by a favoured author. Which words do they use, and how do they use them? How did they organise their plot, characters, settings and dialogue? Adapt what you read, into a form that feels comfortable for you.

Does your plot involve a couple key characters? A common approach found in books: do your chapters switch between the pair and what they are doing? Don't confuse a reader unintentionally. Double-check the continuity of what unfolds for each character; bridge the interval where necessary to ensure that a reader isn't left behind, wondering what (s)he missed.

What you write evolves from choices, decisions made: this rather than that, a preferred topic or subject, a particular slant or reader targeted. One decision leads to another, can condition others to follow. No two writers approach a scene or situation the same way. That's what provides readers with captivating variety.

Settle on the tone or attitude, writing style and story pacing that best suits you and your tale.

Content: more formal, relaxed or comic?

Be consistent in viewpoint and delivery.

Selections made, reconsider descriptions and characterisations.

Two fiction authors—Hammond Innes and Desmond Bagley, a pair of Brit writers—provided inspiration for my three novels. Both offered good stories with plots that flowed well. Conflict. Action. Foreign settings. Crafted detail. Not sure I measured up in that latter category, but...

My current favourite: Wilbur Smith. His novels are largely set in South Africa. The opening of his 1970 book, *Gold Mine*: 'It began in the time when the world was young, in the time before man, in the time before life itself had evolved upon this planet. The crust of the earth was still thin and soft, distorted and riven by the enormous pressure from within.'

Great stuff!

While in no way do I wish to suggest that my efforts share the stature of Wilbur Smith's work, for contrast, the opening of my third novel: '*Why do I wish I were dead?* (paragraph ->) Beyond the steamy sheet of glass looking out on a street, beleaguered people rushed by, doing their best to shield themselves from the elements. It was pissing down, had being doing so for days. By contrast, within the small and trendy eatery located on the fringe of Melbourne's theatre district, it was warm and cozy. Happy couples chatted at most tables. Soft music and the flickering glow of wall sconces only enhanced a decidedly amiable atmosphere.'

What do you think? Decent? Lacking? If the latter, how would you improve it?

Be aware of libel, making defamatory remarks in writing that intrude upon or offend someone's reputation. If in doubt, check what's intended with someone knowledgeable or run it by a lawyer. If uncomfortable with an item, abandon it.

And do remember that a failure to divulge the source of words and ideas found in the writing of others may amount to plagiarism. Ethics demand that the source of material heavily utilized be acknowledged. For sure, direct quotes or lifting out sections of what someone else has written and dropping it into your work without providing obvious credit is a definite no-no.

But there's an enormous grey area. What constitutes common knowledge? Words and ideas arise, evolve over years and it's often impossible to determine ownership or an original source. Clichés for example—who dreamed those up? Anyway, it's best to be aware of the potential problem and avoid having it distort your efforts.

I once used a short poem in an article that was published. When I first spotted the poem it was identified as 'author unknown' or 'source unknown' and, accepting that as read, that's how I identified it in my piece. Was that the right thing to do?

Working Atmosphere

At the outset, decide whether or not a working routine is required. Some writers need discipline and must set aside blocks of writing time. Others work better depending upon impulse or a keen desire to get on with it. Writing can't really be forced. Is writer's block imagined or an actual hindrance? Give some thought to the matter and determine what works best for you, will be most productive.

In my case, I try to press myself to get on with it, but on some days I'm just not in the mood. Then I do something else, hoping that the urge will soon return. On days I'm writing I try to do that before tackling other computer-related chores.

Organise a decent working space and proper tools (room or corner, furniture, computer, how-to books, supplies) before diving into the endeavour. A permanent setup, with needed materials close to hand, is preferable to one that must be organised each time you are keen to write. There's something comforting about sitting down and working in a familiar setting.

Decide what you want or expect to achieve and give thought to what you must invest to get there. A decent manuscript that will become a book that someone will want to read, maybe even buy, or merely something to be shared with family and friends?

Since I don't use my computer everyday, early morning hours on off-days are often devoted to page-revision sessions. Armed with a cup of green tea, I attack pages with a red pen; some days more viciously than others. That morning's batch completed, I reward my efforts, by reading a book until encouraged to tackle some other awaiting chore for that day. For me, not working on the computer every day adds enthusiasm to keying sessions, hopefully improves the quality of what's produced during the hours spent facing the computer's monitor.

Nowadays most writers do their work on a computer. Keyboards, monitors and boxes with flashing lights have made writing easier in so many ways. While depending upon built-in spelling (squiggly red underscores) and grammar (squiggly green underscores) checkers and what's found in a thesaurus may be tempting, it's unwise. Built-in text measuring rules may or may not accommodate the particular context involved. Using a built-in thesaurus, suggested synonyms may not be equivalent, with one or two of the lot being a more appropriate choice. If in doubt, seek clarification in a dictionary.

I find all three aids helpful and use what's reported for the first two as a flag suggesting that I should at least reconsider what I'd written. As for a thesaurus, I'd not be able to get along without its assistance in unearthing an elusive word, the best one for that sentence within that paragraph.

Some twenty years ago I added a thesaurus to WordStar, a wordprocessor I clung to for far too many years. Invoked by a keyboard combination, that thesaurus, as I recall it success in offering a suitable word, surpassed what I now find in MS Word.

For some, onscreen editing works great. For others, nothing beats sitting back with a cup of whatever and applying a red pen to hardcopy. Pages duly annotated, it's back to the computer to make file corrections. Print it again and back to the red pen. How many repeats? Two? Five? However many times it takes to get it right!

There are programs that will assess computer text files and report on content. Some are better than others. I've used a few in the past and the better ones are mentioned in this book.

The internet provides easy access to wads of information, perhaps too much at times to wade through. But, what can now be obtained in minutes used to take hours back when material had to be extracted from books, magazines or loose material; by photocopy or in scribbled notes.

For best internet-search results, narrow the quest criteria to isolate the good stuff. Check your favourite search engine (Google, Alta Vista, Yahoo, whatever) for the best means to focus the search (quotation marks around text, use of + or − sign?).

Suitable material located: within EDIT, click/drag for a portion or SELECT ALL, COPY (to clipboard) and then PASTE into an opened file and FILE > SAVE the file. Notepad comes with Windows (can be added to the Desktop) and doesn't interact with the internet, as does MS Word.

Alternately, on the keyboard (depress the first key and tap second): click/drag for a portion or [Ctrl]+[A] to select all, [Ctrl]+[C] to copy to clipboard, [Ctrl]+[V] to paste into an opened file, [Ctrl]+[S] to save the named file.

Another way to accumulate helpful material is to become your own clipping service. Extract items of interest from magazines, newspapers or newsletters for writers: try danpoynter@parapublising.com (US) or contact press@windshift.bc.ca (Can). Or with the help of a search engine seek other writing-related newsletters and helpful websites.

At home, computer off and resting, tidbits come to mind and those I scribble on scraps of paper. Out and about, scrounged obsolete business cards serve that purpose. Notes from both sources are piled by the computer to await the next onscreen session, or they are pinned to a bulletin board for future consideration. An idea can pop up at any time and, unrecorded, it can be lost forever. At my age, I don't depend upon remembering anything.

To get a better idea of how others work at the craft, obtain a copy of *The Canadian Writer's Guide*. It's filled with great information, suggestions and ideas. If possible get your own copy (even if an older edition) and read it with a highlighter in hand. Most of the writing helpmates I own are adorned with yellow stripes and margin notations.

Being able to submit material electronically has made life so much easier. With nothing to mail, at least at the outset, writers are able to reduce costs that used to prove crippling.

In past years, writers sent out material, hoping for a positive response, one that often never materialised. I once sent a typescript to an agent. And what did I get for the effort involved? The shipping cost was almost twenty dollars and I never received a response to follow-up queries. I can't recall if what I sent was an only copy; if so, that wasn't too bright.

If your book is to be published by a traditional publishing firm, submitting a manuscript on a floppy disk, CD or DVD may be all that's needed...initially. If self-publishing is the chosen route, much more will be required of you.

For instance, bookshops, libraries, other buyers and demanding readers will have to be persuaded to part with cash or dig out the plastic—by you. Refer to the section on self-publishing for related detail.

Generally, for titles on covers, author's name and that of a publisher, a sans serif (no little bits attached to letters) font serves well. For the teaser on the back cover, a serif font (as text inside) is more the standard and, a decent size, is easier to read.

For two novels self-published, on the cover of one I used bold Comic Sans, for the other bold Arial. For both, the font I used for interior text was Bookman Old Style, 10-point, 12-point for the first page inside and on the back cover.

Ten-point Bookman Old Style used to be my computer default font. For this book I chose Bookman Old Style 11-point, together with Comic Sans (differing sizes) as the sans serif font. Perhaps I'll use the same font sizes and that combination for future books.

In deciding which font and size to use, consider potential readers/buyers. For instance, anticipating seniors as readers, a larger font is preferable. Maybe that's why this wrinkly (a Brit term for a senior), not yet in need of 12 or 14, increased his default font from 10-point to 11...

Beyond cover and interior fonts to sort out there are chapter numbers, headers and footers to consider. My last novel had chapter numbers in a 40-point sans serif font. Headers were in the same sans serif font used on the cover but smaller (9-point), with the content differing according to the page. For those even numbered (left facing): page number - author name. For odd numbered pages (right facing): book title - page number.

Layout

Some writers plan ahead. Others forge ahead. Each expects that somehow all will come together at some point. Some writers start off with an outline of what's intended, others do not. Outlining programs and schemes are available—check on the internet.

Declining an outliner, a spreadsheet program like Excel works best for me. My layout page for a book includes structuring notes at the top and chapter content notes below (see following example). Columns gather the number pages for book portions (word counts could be added). At the base of the page, the 8.5 x 11 inch typescript page total is converted (by an Excel formula) to the number of anticipated pages for a 5.5 x 8.5 inch book-page format: double or so. Margin settings, pages beyond those numbered and added blank space on a page affect the extent of the page number increase.

A layout sheet example, COMING UP SHORT (info only, not part of book structure):
- size - 5.5 x 8.5 inches
- text - 10pt Bookman OS
- interior - headers/9pt Arial
- chap#s - 48pt Arial (bold) on line 4
- prolog.chaps.epilog text starts - line 12
- cover: koala top of Asian street scene, blue + green background, title in bold Arial letters
- A novel by... - bold sans serif solid letters + same for spine

- first-pg - 3-book summary, back: cover credit (if any), disclaimer, dedication, prev books, contact info, books, contact info
- title-pg - title, author, publisher, back: publication data
- manuscript pages - keep total number under 185?

pages

		pages
prolog	+ first/title pages	5
chap1	Aust: Steve, Charlie/GraceS.	4
chap2	Japan: Steve and Jigoro	9
chap3	Aust: flashback/Charlie	6
chap4	Japan: Steve/Kamakura visit	8
chap5	Aust: Steve arrives	7

~~~~~~

chap20	Steve/outback --> to Hong Kong	7
chap21	Steve in Hong Kong	7
chap22	Steve in Hong Kong	7
chap23	Steve escapes, heads for Greece	7
chap24	Steve on Crete, to stay	5
last-pg	about author	
cvr-bk	this book outlined	

Manscr ttls: pages ----->	168
Convert: mnscr2book --->	?

Last update: 15oct06

Beyond printing cost considerations for the number of pages, a post office will charge extra (big time) for a book that doesn't fit through a slot in its plastic guide. Soft cover assumed, consider using thinner paper if excess thickness is anticipated. And don't forget to allow for package wrapping. Before completing your book, try a few similar books for thickness (280 pages or so a fit?) at a post office outlet.

I first based the typescript to book-size conversion calculation at the bottom of the sheet on a previous book's results. Because I altered the structure, that calculation ended up well off and I had to adopt plan B: thinner paper for the book. The thinner pages were a decided improvement, aside from postal savings. They improved the look and feel of the final product, proved to be easier on the book's binding.

If you compiled your manuscript on a computer with chapters or sections as separate files for easier handling, the various portions will eventually have to be combined into one large file. If you are self-publishing the book, that large file will have to be converted, using Adobe Acrobat or other PDF-creating means (check on internet). Printers require a PDF (portable document format) file. For more on creating such files, refer to the later PDF preparation section.

Throughout the project ensure that all book sections are well backed up—both during the creation of the typescript and before proceeding with a PDF conversion. I know people who failed to duplicate, back up, their work and lost it all when a computer failed. There's no such thing as excessive backup!

Declining any sort of comprehensive computer backup, I copy book sections to a floppy disk and a CD as files as created or altered, as I do for other computer files I create. Periodically I bundle book files using WinZip and store that compressed bundle apart from the computer. Unfortunately 3.5-inch floppy drives are vanishing, as I discovered with a recent laptop acquisition—guess I'll have to rethink that one...

All this promotion of backup may sound a bit like overkill but storage media do fail and I have no wish to waste countless hours recreating material that could have been easily protected earlier. Only last week I tried to access a floppy disk and was unable to do so. However, the disk content list appeared onscreen and I was able to reconstruct the files on another disk extracted from my stock of such aging media.

What's Good...and Not

Basic to good writing: Use active voice rather than passive. 'He decided...' rather than 'It was decided by him.' 'Perfection requires added effort.' rather than 'Added effort is required to achieve perfection.'

Be on the lookout for repetition, words or content. For effect it may prove helpful but unintended it will alienate readers.

Sloppy writing—an accumulation of errors or wandering about and not respecting the original objective—is a book killer, a reader turnoff.

As frequently repeated, what you write must please a reader, offer something entertaining or contribute something of value. Your efforts can't be boring or a mere rehash of what's appeared in other books. It needs to be fresh and filled with vibrant words, gripping nouns and verbs. It must stimulate a reader's emotions or cater to her or his interests.

Try using understatement as opposed to exaggeration, or just say what's needed, in words that best do the job.

Introduce the unexpected.

Brevity has it place and always should be kept in mind, despite the fact that there are times when brevity isn't what's best.

Clarity is ever important, as is harmony: a smooth and proper blending of ingredients.

Know your subject or topic and check all related facts.

Keep an eye on structure and grammar.

Share your perspective. Show how you feel about a topic and, if it fits, display a bit of attitude.

Mix action and more peaceful interludes. Life is not all get up and go. Is yours? Mine's not. Pacing is important. Characters need to move and interact but everyone must pause for reflection at some point. No-one can be gung ho 24/7/52.

Most people work, in one way or another. What they do and describing how they do it adds reality to a story. Don't overlook the best parts of a job description but detail the activity in moderation.

And what about those pages unnumbered, those beyond chapters or sections? Most novels provide a glimpse of what's inside, on the back cover or on the first page inside the book. Or that first page may duplicate a chapter excerpt. Or it may display a favourable review or two. The backsides of that first page and the title page can also serve. A dedication, disclaimer or contact information for one, publication data for the other. What's included or excluded and what goes where can vary, can be somewhat shifted about; check out how other books handle such requirements.

As shown below for a previous novel, the dedication appeared on the back of the first page. The publisher's name and where the book was printed appear on the back of the title page. For this book the dedication, first added to the end of the intro section, was later shifted to adopt what was done for a previous book. The publisher and where the book was printed was shifted to the foot of the title page.

For my last novel:

On the back of the first page –

While some authors might believe that novels are created in isolation, that's truly not the case. Along the way many people contribute to the end result, knowingly or not, in small ways and larger. Those helping me know who they are and I thank them.

Like my previous books, this one is dedicated to family, life's enduring support, and in particular to two women who've enhanced my life. Adele, sadly no longer with us. And Tracey who brightens my days...

Also by Donald Gordon:
Shattered Expectations
No More Illusions

For information:
tradon@islandnet.com

On the Back of the title page –

Copyright 2006 © Donald G. Wilkes
All rights reserved. No portion of this book may be reproduced or transmitted in any form or means whatsoever, excepting short passages for review, without the prior permission in writing from the publisher.

This novel is a work of fiction. Any resemblance between depicted characters or names, places or locales, incidents or events, entities or actual persons, living or dead, is unintentional or coincidental.

Library and Archives Canada Cataloguing in Publication
Gordon, Donald, 1935-
Coming Up Short
Donald Gordon.
ISBN 0-9737633-1-0I. Title.
PS8613.O73C65 2006 C813'.6 C2006-906016-9

Abbey Isle Publishing
Printed in Victoria, Canada

Manuscript (1)

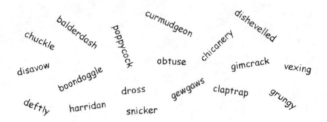

Although much of what follows is applicable to other forms of writing, this section and the next (as do most others) lean toward creating fictional material, a novel in particular. And the intent is not just getting a bunch of words onto paper! No, the goal is to produce a manuscript one can be proud of, something duly completed but not the polished wonder one should expect after a proper professional editing. The objective is to create material worthy of showing to others, an effort that will hopefully satisfy those with a critical eye. Editing, an extension of the revision process, is something few writers do well on their own.

Many books have been written about writing and I have no wish to or intention of duplicating what's already been admirably covered in a host of helpful books, such as *The Canadian Style* and *A writer's*

Handbook of Current English. And yet there are several fundamental items worth repeating; aspects of writing frequently overlooked or misused, bits and pieces that cannot be mentioned too many times.

Although few of us have had a life worth writing about, we all have background incidents that can be worked into fiction. Make a note of such occurrences, whether yours or those of others. Who knows what might prove handy? Maintain a tidbit file and tuck notes into it. Rummage through those notes from time to time for ideas or snippets than might fit a current project. And, don't discard any written material presently found unsuitable—one day it might just fit the bill. Out and about, always carry a notepad and pen. Watch and listen to what's going on around you; good ideas may be lurking.

If you expect others to be attracted to your work, what you write must first matter to you. A lot. But it also has to be of potential interest to readers. What to write about; what's worthy? Start with what you know, find familiar and comfortable. Upfront choose a genre and stay within its confines, as exhibited by others who've successfully exploited the genre: mystery, historical, children, young teens, romance, sci-fi, adventure, thriller.

At the outset be prepared to produce a middling product, even after doing your best and tackling a rewrite or three. Practice does indeed make perfect, or at least provide improvement, and everyone cannot be a winner, particularly early in the game. *Middling* is better than *mediocre* or material even less appealing or satisfying.

To get a better idea of what constitutes a decent typescript, browse books that appear similar to what you want to produce, wish to end up with. Check library shelves and those in bookshops. Watch for and evaluate style and structure, catchy characters or plot themes, subtle hooks, sex or violence content if that's where you're headed. As previously stated, I found my initial inspiration for my three published novels in books by Desmond Bagley and Hammond Innes who created adventure tales set in what we'd consider foreign settings. For my three novels I involved locales discovered on trips I'd taken: Greece, Turkey, Grenada, Cuba, Japan, Hong Kong, Australia.

But novels don't have to be set elsewhere. Everyone doesn't travel afar. Many topnotch books involve spots closer to home. Some books tell the tale within an extended time period and others deal with a relatively brief period.

Got a favourite author or two? Without 'borrowing' (read that as stealing) actual text, note what works well: phrasing, structure and style, dialogue, pacing, setting and character detailing. For an example of getting good mileage from fewer words, browse one of Sue Grafton' s detective novels (A is for... B is for...). Wilbur Smith, my favourite fiction writer, writes admirable books, most of which are set in southern Africa.

Dedicated writers are likely avid readers. Aside from actually putting pen to paper (or fingers to keyboard), how better can you learn the craft? Exploring examples of a chosen genre represents research and that may well prove more helpful than taking a general writing course. Read, read and then read some more. Find out how those who've preceded you have utilised their words, how they organised their structure.

Although a general writing course may be debatable, taking a focused writing course or two could pay significant dividends. Say, one on dialogue or another on revision and editing. Or check out self-help books; there are lots of those available, some more worthy than others. I've acquired several and refer to them from time to time, although less so now than earlier on.

Basic helpmates to have sitting by the computer or shelved nearby:

- dictionary and thesaurus (both substantial in size)
- enduring standards like Zinsser's *On Writing Well* and Strunk and White's *Elements of Style*
- *Fowlers Modern English Usage,* despite it being a bit difficult to wade through at times

Other writing aids I found particularly helpful:

- *How to Write Realistic Dialogue,* Jean Saunders (Allison & Busby)
- *Conflict, Action & Suspense,* William Noble (Writer's Digest)
- *Self-Editing for Fiction Writers,* Renni Browne and Dave King (HarperPerennial)
- *Revising Fiction,* David Madden (Plume)
- *Getting the Words Right,* Theodore A Rees Cheney (Writer's Digest)

Similar helpmates can be found in libraries and larger bookshops (browse before buying) but you'll have to hunt for specific books or, more likely, have to order them. Focus on specific areas of writing (dialogue, self-editing, conflict, suspense) where you feel deficient. For those wishing to add a little spice to the brew, check out Elizabeth Benedict's *The Joy Of Writing Sex* (Story Press) or *Writing Erotic Fiction* by Mike Bailey (Teach Yourself Books).

But such exploration, tracking down writing helpmates, is passive. Why not get more active? Join a writing group, a writing workshop or other gatherings of scribes. Hear what others have produced. Read aloud what you've written and seek a critique. I belong to two such groups and have profited enormously from feedback received.

With paragraphs representing an army division, sentences are its battalions. Both need to be a logical bundling of words, those being the troops needed to win a war, in this case the hoped-for battle outcome being an impressive creation.

Words, sentences and paragraphs require focused organisation, structuring and logical grouping. Introduce a new paragraph as context shifts. Add a blank line or two, or move to a new chapter, to indicate a significant change in setting, situation or character, or time—be that a plot advancement or flashback (peek into the past).

My first pass at creating chapters shoots for haphazard content heading toward a decent number of manuscript pages (6 or so?). I need to get those ideas out of my head and into a computer file. Eventually they arrive on a printed page, there to be attacked with a red pen in search of areas to correct or improve. Pages liberally slashed and annotated, it's back to the computer to try to make sense of all that red-penned stuff. Some manuscript pages and sections require considerably more revision sessions than others.

Aspiring writers need a routine that they feel comfortable with. Revision and editing onscreen may suffice for some. Other scribes benefit more from printing pages and then attacking them.

Reading pages aloud better pinpoints what's amiss, more clearly indicates what needs extra attention. For me, reading already-revised material at one of my writing groups always brings to light glitches or more serious transgressions missed earlier. That's how I screen chapter portions and completed articles bound for a seniors' column.

For a first typescript pass, concentrate on getting basic chapter material semi-organised, grouped into logical clumps. And while it may prove hard to do, try to ignore spelling, grammar, syntax and logic or any revision or polishing considerations. Just get all those thoughts onto paper or into a computer file, before they go astray.

To avoid having to later delete a footer/header, don't number manuscript pages.

During earlier passes, expand content and seek obvious improvement in character and setting descriptions. Watch for glaring grammar errors and spelling mistakes. Curtail clichés. Trim any excessive explanation or what appears blatant padding.

Introduce, expand or revise dialogue. Substitute it for narrative where it'll do a better job.

Enhance character or setting descriptions by adding or reducing content, seeking quality, not quantity.

Revamp portions that offend the eye, segments not in keeping with what's intended. For my last novel—to get to the point that I was either satisfied or truly sick of looking at the material—I went through chapters at least six times; for a previous book, a couple more than that. Even with all that, I missed things.

In a later pass through the material, don't forget to check chapters for continuity, a logical combining and flow of the tale and those involved in it.

And throughout the undertaking, don't forget that file backup routine. Make a change; backup the file.

Fonts

Having already browsed library and bookshop shelves for content ideas, give some thought to fonts and sizes. Which best suit the cover concept, title page, interior text, headers or footers, chapter numbers or headings? If you have a publisher or printer in mind, check for fonts favoured by that firm. Some fonts may be more acceptable than others.

Arial and Comic Sans are sans serif fonts (no little bits edging letters) I've used in books for non-text purposes, aside from sub-headings such as appears above. For text I used Bookman Old Style, a serif (little added bits) font, in all three.

If manuscript preparation absorbs much of the time you spend on a computer, you may wish, for general use, to adopt a particular default font and size. Times Roman is popular. I once used Century Schoolbook but that one lost out to Bookman Old Style. If you have a favoured font, one that's doesn't stray too far from what's generally acceptable, ensure that it's suitable for submitting a typescript, if that's what you eventually expect to do.

Paragraph indents (as used herein) I routinely adjust to .25 inch—never did figure out how to alter that default...

Plot

In a novel something must happen. Action moves a tale forward and enlivens the characters. Give thought to what depicted action should generate in terms of reaction or subsequent events, what could or should result from it or be generated because of it.

The plot and how it evolves must be logical and cannot overly depend upon coincidence. Don't assume facts that seem to ring true—first check the details.

Try to avoid abstractions and generalizations that can confuse or disconnect readers. Create anticipation by introducing an unexpected twist. Add a dollop of ambiguity to muddy up a situation. Introduce surprises, mysterious incidents, awkward encounters for characters to deal with and resolve.

Your plot must entertain or excite. Offer page content that will tantalise, thrill or terrify a reader. The words must make a reader want to keep turning pages—that is, after enjoying all that's on each and every one of them. The tale's events need to flow forward to a crisis or climax, and then onward to a resolution.

But, the whole process, in evolving, mustn't appear contrived. Consider what you have created so far, and what that should lead on to. Is all of it what one could expect to find in real life?

Character depiction choices must fit comfortably within setting and situation descriptions. Disclose and expand upon the nature or attitude of characters through their actions and what happens to them. Consider employing a flashback to flesh out a

81

character or introduce a subplot, if doing so will enhance the tale without confusing a reader.

Setting

Where and how characters interact fleshes out fiction: a face-off in a seedy bar, lost in a dense jungle, trapped in an out-of-control plane, arguing in an elegant room. Is there someplace else (s)he would rather be at a particular point in time? How does a character feel about her or his current situation or location, past or roots?

Settings sorted, avoid excessive description by introducing what's needed in bits and pieces, as needed to keep pace with what characters are doing. Let them experience, interact with, work or play within the surroundings. Use actual place names, or a comparison to another that's named, to enhance descriptions.

Enhance, spice up, setting details. For example, if in a city, bring in a seedy café, a grubby street, massive construction site, a rundown hotel or an upper-crust dwelling. Perhaps some green space.

Be specific in choosing nouns. Instead of car, say Ford. Rather than use fruit, say apple. Instead of room, say dungeon or garret. Substitute rose for flower. Employ brand names to boost the framing of the tale within which characters must evolve.

Don't overburden readers. Give them enough environment detail to encourage them to employ their imagination. Don't tell them what's obvious or repeat what they already have heard or know, or should easily understand.

Use comparison and contrast, analogy, allusion, similes and metaphors to enhance content. Illustrate likeness between items, ideas or characters. But, use such devices sparingly and eliminate those judged less effective. Occasional use of alliteration (adjacent words, same first letter) may also prove helpful. See the earlier section on words for expanded detail on these items.

Characters

Readers should love, like, dislike or hate your characters, who need to deal with complications or compelling situations.

A good character, one bound to make a lasting impression on a reader, must be believable and fit within the tale. (S)he should be enchanting, intriguing, repugnant or whatever best addresses the circumstances. Define your actors by appearance, diction, attitude or actions, normal or odd mannerisms.

Why not contrast differences to make it easier for readers to distinguish one character from another. A weak one core to the tale, introduce someone strong. One commendable, another not. One tall, the other short. Bulky versus slim. Older and younger. One strong-willed, the other weak. Normal versus oddball. Subdued and outrageous. Augment someone natty by bringing in someone scruffy. The main character a wolf, have a sheep to be pounced upon.

Don't introduce more characters than needed for the tale to properly unfold or too many at any one time.

Is the first character appearing properly and adequately introduced? Does her or his name suit the intended portrayal? Is it a name that'll be remembered? Does (s)he show attitude or emotion, provide sufficient stimulation for readers to get better acquainted? A protagonist needs an antagonist, one also impressive. Introduce a dominant character trait for one or the other or both. Is there some kind of a personal relationship, a shared past or common vocation?

Characterisation should develop gradually, more from actions and use of dialogue than narrative. Choose character traits that introduce or hint at attitude, ethnic origin, social status or whatever. Why not choose a name that suggests a character trait. For instance, William Faulkner, in one of his books, chose the name Snopes for a conniving individual. A good choice? Does that identification work for you?

The interplay between characters must ensure that inter-relationships are clearly understood, that the association makes sense and is enhanced by a crafted blending of background and attitude, dress, striking features, deportment, needs, desires, quirks or manner of voice.

Introduce emotion: hate, love, anger, sulking, envy. Reacting to frustration. Blaming anyone else inappropriately. Heading for the bottle. Throwing in the towel. Seeking revenge.

Introduce a bit of body language, a response or prelude, to dialogue: tears, clenched fists, a grimace, a reddening face.

Appearance: Clothing does more than just cover a body. It can depict social standing, employment, economic success or failure, regional roots, an emotional state, a character's self image or an attitude. Exploit how characters perceive or react to clothing, their own or what others wear. In deciding on garb, bear in mind that reader reaction to dress may differ. For some the impact is strong. With others, garb may matter little.

Characters unfold in numerous ways, including by way of dialogue or monologue, the latter either internal or external. Let a reader find out how they feel about one another or themselves or a situation, through what they say, or how it's delivered: whisper, shout, menacing tone, a snide remark. Introduce a heated argument to divulge participant characteristics, whether an isolated incident or one ongoing.

Where do characters come from? Friends or intriguing people encountered, whether admired or detested. Aspects of yourself. Family members. Impressive historical figures. Individuals encountered while reading. All adapted and brought to life with reasonable chunks of narrative, spoken words, actions or body language; with or without a bit of background sketching.

Why not reveal one character through the eyes, actions or reactions of another.

In detailing a character, consider these:

- Body: stocky, frail, deformed, shrivelled.
- Voice: raucous, mellow, muffled
- Face: cheerful, agitated, pensive. Lips: tremulous, unsmiling, set, odd features
- Eyes: downcast, twinkling, mischievous
- Hair: colour, bobbed, braided, thick
- Attire: drab, natty, outrageous, gaudy

Do your characters yearn for what they don't have or should they? Captivating novels revolve around challenges, confrontations, surprises, personal threats and how characters handle them.

Expand character personas by placing participants somewhere. Or have them involved in doing something odd or dangerous. If suitable, depict a dull life or disclose personal complications that clamour for clarification.

Work character details into the text bit by bit, sufficient at any one time to keep things moving, to satisfy the current requirements of the tale. Holding something back for the right moment can recapture waning reader interest.

Avoid mundane or superfluous detail unless satisfied that it's truly needed to properly define a character.

Ensure that your characters differ one from another; that each acts and speaks in keeping with what would be expected in real life for such a person.

Are your characters consistent in speech and behaviour? If not, why not? Clarify any deviations introduced to accommodate the tale's requirements.

Create character-depicting names. Struggling to come up with what to call them? Track down names (in bulk) via the internet: an association listing, a roster of sports types or famous folk or actors, whatever. I found a whole page (a foreign association listing) and reduced it to just the names that I could adapt as needed.

What kind of character does a moniker like Archibald bring to mind? Alphonse? Or Hammond? How about referring to minor characters by actions, function or appearance: Drag Ass, Overalls or Old Dusty for a farm hand, Greaseball for a lowlife?

Avoid confusing the reader with handles that sound too much alike. Readers need to be able to distinguish between the players. Don't twin first names like Ted and Fred, Bart and Albert, Jack and John or Nora and Norma. Instead, adopt such as Ethel and Rebecca, Bert and Peter, Tom and Martin, Virginia and Shirley. The same applies to last names. A name selected, can it be improved through modification?

Use first names or last? Both when a character's first mentioned? Last names more often identify character in stories, but using a first name (more casual, less formal?) may better fit within a tale. Add a Mr, Mrs or Ms? What suits the tale's framework: formality, exaggeration of one character's social standing or position in the pecking order? First names could indicate a closer association or friendship.

In my novels I prefer first names for key characters. For those they encountered, the choice depends upon the interplay. First, for those closer. Last, for others less involved or acting in other than a friendly way. Switching between one and the other could be used to reduce repetition.

In choosing a name consider: background, occupation or physical appearance (condition, physical disabilities, scars or other defining markings), peculiar dress or manner, ethnic origin, actions or how a character communicates. How about a peculiar mannerism: eye twitching, repeated hand activity, foot tapping?

Does a character's speech match her or his depiction?

Sex is a life component. If it fits, use it, bearing in mind what's acceptable and not for an intended audience. What have you found or preferred in books you've read? What did you find objectionable? Did sex add reality to the characters? Was it overdone, excessively detailed? Would you write it differently? If so, how?

What type of speech to use? Choose with care and don't overdo any dialect. Some writers adhere to a belief that it should only be used when the character is first encountered and not continued. Respect any dialect used by ensuring that it fits the particular character involved and how that character participates in the plot.

A professional voice may please a reader employed in a professional capacity but may not appeal to other readers you want to reach. A rural choice may alienate city folk. A heavy dialect may irritate readers, as could a bland character depiction. Blending characters within a story is best, as long as each and every one of them moves the tale forward.

Point of View

Who is the story about and who will tell it, firsthand or second? A first person perspective (I) limits the tale to what the speaker knows or sees. Third person (she or he, a character name) provides greatest flexibility.

Which is best for the tale you wish to tell? Is your choice valid for how the plot unfolds? First or third, ensure that the point of view is consistent, that any departures are properly handled.

Third person more common and first person often effective, omniscient (narrator knows all) is less often used; is more difficult to work with.

Shifting between points of view may work within a book if properly handled. I just read a book wherein chapters for the bad guy were in first person and the rest in third. But switching about in a short story or a defined segment of a tale, due to space dictates, may not. Don't confuse readers.

Dialogue

Next to using words properly and effectively, dialogue can make or break a piece of writing. The success of a novel may well hinge upon the words exchanged between characters. Writers are frequently judged by dialogue found in their books. Is yours fresh and gripping? Make sure that your exchanges measure up, that what characters say, and how they say it, will entertain readers.

Good dialogue defines and breathes life into characters. A depiction of discourse, it shifts context to the immediate. Readers want lots of it. Perhaps not half of the content but they'll want and expect a chunk not far short of that.

Some readers open a book and check random pages—insufficient good dialogue found, goodbye book! Why not open a prologue or the first chapter with a bit of gripping dialogue to grab that reader's attention.

Dialogue isn't real conversation, but it's intended to emulate an exchange, portray what's found in an actual discussion. Find out how other writers, those who have achieved a measure of success, deal with exchanges between characters.

A monologue is half a conversation, is one person not talking to another. Or it could involve someone assumed to be present, a person not necessarily evident to the reader. Why not employ some internal monologue to display or round out a character's feelings or attitude.

Interior or exterior monologue can be effective...if it fits. Don't confuse dialogue and internal monologue. If using the latter, brief is better, without quotation marks and italics employed only where needed for added clarity. Whether correct or not, for internal monologue I use italics only if using *I* or *me* in the text.

To distinguish an aside from monologue, set it in italics.

Attributes (person named or (s)he said) should be doled out with care but are essential where who's speaking may be unclear.

Is your dialogue appropriate for the speaker, station in life, age, nationality, period or setting? Children speak differently than adults. Education, occupation and lifestyle affect speech. Dialect could reflect an ethnic origin or a minority societal position.

Dialogue enlivens a tale, provided the exchanges aren't overloaded, weak or flabby. Don't burden it with worn out nouns or verbs, off-putting adjectives or adverbs. Listen to how real people talk to one another and then decide how what was discovered can be translated, converted, into your dialogue.

Employ vibrant discourse in place of plodding narrative. Let characters describe what they see and hear rather than just telling readers what they need to know. Anger or another emotion is more vivid if brought out in what one character says and how another responds.

Much of what readers learn about a protagonist or antagonist, or others, should come from speech. Backgrounds. Beliefs. Interests. Attitudes. Emotions. Foibles. Use dialogue to display how one character feels about another or relates to an incident. Avoid meaningless drivel.

Single quotation marks or double? Both are used. Take your pick. As indicated in following examples, I prefer the double for dialogue and save the single choice for what might be introduced into what is being said, or to highlight a word or phrase.

Effective and concise exchanges the goal, make each and every word work and move things forward. Are words used as verbal weapons, cast in anger or desperation or is it a joyful exchange?

Why not add to dialogue bits of action, before, after or within a speaker's contribution. An example: "No more," he said, shifting awkwardly. Crisp beats— injected action associated with what's being said— can define a moment or crank up tension. It can vary the dialogue rhythm; clarify characters, tone or attitude. A foot tapping. A frown. Eyes rolled. A finger wagged.

Variety in structure improves the flow of exchanges, can make them seem more real.

Cull out lazy, filler or phoney dialogue (How are you? Fine. And you?).

Why not try a speech signature like 'old sport' to distinguish a speaker by ethnic origin.

Add a dollop of narrative to break up an extended exchange.

Adopt standalone dialogue if the speaker is clear. Not so, add a *she said* or *he said* to clarify the speaker; most readers hardly notice those attributes. Include a character's name within a response of another to clarify the participants.

To lessen the impact of a needed drawn out speech, introduce snippets of action or explanatory narrative or an interjection by the other participant in the exchange. But, adding too many chunks of interruption can degrade dialogue and reduce its effectiveness. Strive for the right balance.

Engaging dialogue enhances character definition and drama development, adds fuel to what drives a tale onward, toward a climax or crisis.

Brief spurts of dialogue can suggest tension, without over-employing exclamation marks.

Stimulate tension, potential conflict or hint at what may yet come to pass, by having someone say one thing while thinking something else. Example: "Tell me about...," he said, while mentally removing her clothing piece by piece.

Employ contractions, as we tend to do in actual conversation (it's, can't, don't).

Actions do often speak louder than words. Demonstrate rather than just tell.

Don't add to *(s)he said*, adverbs like *breathlessly*—change the verb. Don't say: "I can't buy that,'" Stan said *stubbornly*. Better (with or without a 'Stan said,'): "No, it's just not on. No way, forget it!"

Scrutinise words ending in *ly*. Needed? Would other phrasing work better?

Avoid phrases such as '...she grinned' or '...John barked' unless the verb choice is truly better there than not.

All done? Satisfied with what you've assembled? Read the dialogue aloud—does it still work, sound natural? Any changes needed? Reworking discourse produces better dialogue, perhaps even brilliant exchanges. Write and assess. Revise and reassess. Scrutinise and alter once again if need be. And then, more of the same...until it's the best you are able to produce. For inspiration, if you can get your hands on a copy, you may wish to browse *How to Write Realistic Dialogue* by Joan Saunders.

And how should dialogue appear on a page? Some maintain that each new comment or speaker should be positioned as a new paragraph (best for clarity?). Others mix dialogue within a paragraph, along with some narrative or bits of action. Whichever works best for you, ensure that who's speaking is clear. Which of the following appeals to you?

"...now?"
She shrugged her shoulders. "Why not?"
–or-
"...now?"
She shrugged her shoulders.
"Why not?"
I favour the first version.

On to the second section on this topic...

Manuscript (2)

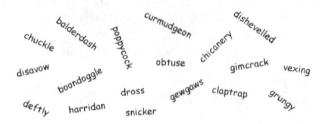

When is a manuscript truly finished? You've written and rewritten and, as best you can judge, the existing content represents your best effort. In other words, it's as good as it's going to get. Maybe not truly completed, but hopefully ninety percent plus. Who could ask for more? Is it now the time to launch your creation? Maybe yes...maybe no.

Actually a book is never ever really finished. It'll always remain a work in progress, something that could always could be improved, in one way or another, to one degree or another. But at some point a halt must be called, whatever the lingering misgivings. It's time to wrap it up and get it into print—if that's the intention. Anyway, by now, you may well be unable to manage another run through it.

Once in print, it's best not to read the material again, in whole or part. Why agonize over something discovered that begs to be changed if a reprinting isn't contemplated?

Is creating a decent typescript (30% writing/inspiration?) the most important part of getting a book into print? Perhaps, but much goes on between the initial and subsequent manuscript passes and being able to hold a printed book in your hand. For instance, rewrite (70% revision/perspiration?) is essential, perhaps repeated several times over. Successful writers invest rewrite time to varying degrees in the interest of achieving a better than acceptable typescript. Or, they arrange to have someone else share that burden.

Few authors have equalled the reputed measure of Timothy Findley. Created in longhand, his manuscripts were converted by his companion into printed pages on a computer's printer. According to what I understand, the submitted material flowed through to publication unchanged. How many scribes ever managed that? How many even contemplated such an achievement?

In the interest of delivering a manuscript that'll receive a positive reception, to whatever extent considered proper, respect the interests and sensitivity of your target audience. Fail to do that and disaster, rejection, will soon come to pass.

What do readers want, something chronological or a tale that logically shifts about, moves smoothly along and properly shifts between scenes and characters? Don't confuse that reader who was persuaded to open your book. Invest what's required to plan and execute stunning content within a fitting framework.

A book's opening and closing paragraphs and sentences merit extra attention. They need to hook readers and later leave them satisfied. If you fail to grab readers very early in a tale they'll drift away, go off and look for someone else's book. Leaving readers hanging at the end of a tale fosters frustration, dissuades prospective buyers for future books.

Open with a sentence that's a grabber: a bit of gripping dialogue, a disturbing or intriguing incident or occurrence, perhaps a letter or comment that hints at what's to come. What, who, when or where? Opening examples: 'You did what?' 'I came face to face with...' 'The gross gangster bent forward.' Or something like the start of Joel Ross's prologue for *Eye For An Eye*: 'How long can a petrified fifteen-year-old kneel at her murdered sister's grave after her funeral?'

Ending a book properly is almost as important as starting one. Readers want to be left with a message, a lesson learned or some sense that their time had been well invested. They prefer to be left, happy or sad, having finished a tale neatly wrapped up. They don't want to feel abandoned, left sitting, book in hand, with matters unresolved.

Have you exploited opportunities to introduce action or conflict? Why not throw in a lesser happening to introduce intentional distraction. No tale can survive a lack of action, to whatever extent applicable to the storyline. Readers expect it.

Readers want to encounter someone struggling, with emotions or another character, or within a significant situation. Why not encourage them to anticipate what's yet to come, what will at some point be resolved.

Does your novel contain appropriate suspense or tension? If not, why not? A gripping story holds readers, keeps them turning pages. Drama thrives on escalating doses of suspense. How about adding a dollop of confrontation or uncertainty to move the plot along? Danger. A locked door. Mystery. A dilemma. A burst of emotion. Disagreement. Something a character doesn't want known by others. Pick up the pace with such devices and slow it down by interjecting narrative. Give readers an opportunity to pause and take a breath, in anticipation of more stimulation to follow.

What about a bit of misdirection, something left hanging or unresolved; an uncertainty that encourages a reader to speculate? Something undefined that may or may not be essential to the storyline. A sound heard but not recognised. A light flickering deep within night-dark woods. A briefcase discovered in an unexpected spot. A letter left unopened, leaning against a vase on an ornate table.

Could a subtle or blatant suggestion of what's to come assist your plot? Someone trapped in a dark confined space. An ailment likely to reappear, but when? An appointment made but missed. An awkward promise given, in good faith or not. Such ploys add tension to a tale, keep a reader involved and eager to soak up what's on that page and then move on to the next.

Backup

In constructing a manuscript consider using single-spaced individual chapter or section files. Smaller units are easier to work with and they may better accommodate disk backup storage (floppy disk?). Protect your invested effort. Copy new files or those altered to a floppy disk (becoming history but handy) or a USB/flash drive or a rewritable (-RW) CD or DVD—preferably to two options in case one proves faulty and impossible to access.

Of those options, only the floppy disk represents a storage problem for multiple book files. They may have to be stored on more than one disk. Still a bit tight? For some strange reason, MS Word alters file size on multiple saves. If important, to ensure that file dimensions are the smallest possible, open a file and do something non-altering such as checking the word count. Then save the file again. Did the file shrink? If not, repeat the process to return that file to its previous smaller size and try another file to create some minimal spare space.

Invoke consistent and frequent backup. Adopt and adhere to a routine. Start a new file or make a change; backup the file. Avoid having to recreate your creation in part or all, should you experience a devastating computer failure.

Revising Material

In addition to being easier to handle and backup, moving about a single-spaced file is easier and faster. There's no need later to convert it from double-space to single and if you want to print double-spaced from a single-spaced file, no problem. After first saving it, on the keyboard (hold down first key and tap second): select the text with [ctrl]+[A] and then [ctrl]+[2] to print double-spaced printing, (or +[15] for one and a half spacing). That done, don't save the file or you'll have to return the file to what it was before altering the spacing. Error made, no matter. Replace the file from one of those file backups tucked away.

Much of the rewriting process involves getting rid of words already on the screen or page, with what's remaining then being targeted for improvement. Scrutinise each and every word to ensure that it contributes, that there's not a better word to replace it.

Abandon passive (is/was) phrasing in favour of active. Why say 'It was a lovely day when he left the house.' when you could say 'A lovely day warmed him as he left the house.'

Ensure that pronouns (he, she, they) are properly used, that, as applicable, they do relate to the last person mentioned by name or direct reference.

Be consistent in tense (present, past...) unless a change is called for, is needed to be accurate in the circumstances. Does that change work within the context, whether shifted to a new paragraph or not.

Keep an eye out for spots where italics are needed, where they will help clarify context: foreign words or phrases, word emphasis (what *they* say...), titles, some internal monologue. Use italics sparingly. This topic plus a host of others are admirably covered in *The Canadian Style* or *A Handbook of Current English*.

Effective but best used sparingly: comparison and contrast, allusions, analogies, metaphors and similes. They all deal with a likeness between items. Allusion: an indirect reference. Analogy: introducing an unusual comparison (say, comparing financial shortcomings and battle losses). Metaphor: a figure of speech that implies a comparison between two unlike things. Simile: a metaphor with *like* or *as* added. Perhaps a touch of alliteration (adjacent word starting with the same first letter) could prove handy.

Parody could be another useful tool, for writers better able to understand it and employ it properly and to advantage. It's not something I've attempted. Defined in a dictionary as a feeble imitation, I sought added definition in other books on my shelf but only found clarification in *Fowler's Modern English Usage;* that source offered synonyms such as burlesque, caricature or a travesty in print. I felt no wiser.

Some say that a sentence that cannot be read aloud in one breath is too long. Variety works best. Mix some long sentences and others short or in between. Long sentences tend to slow the pace while short ones pick it up.

Why not throw in the odd one-word or no-verb sentence.

Beyond dialogue, add variety by throwing in a few contractions (you're, don't, he'd).

Avoid repetition unless intended for effect. If intended, double check to ensure that that objective has been achieved.

Curtail the use of exclamation marks, punctuation often added for emphasis or to indicate a shout or the raising of voice in dialogue.

Are your paragraph breaks meaningful and logical? Do they indicate a topic or time shift; a change in setting, character or story activity? Is some sort of transition required to bridge the switch, to clearly indicate a change? Introduce transitional words or phrases (equally important, also, later, next, moreover, even so, meanwhile, nearby, finally). Or a bridging paragraph to provide a reader smooth passage within what's going on.

Do you insert a blank line or two between some paragraphs to emphasise a more extensive shift of scene or passage of time, a significant alteration but not one warranting a new chapter? For a shift even more significant, such as a brief flashback, consider inserting three asterisks (***) with a blank line above and below. Try working a flashback into the manuscript.

Have you noticed that in one book the first line of a new paragraph following a blank line or two is indented and in another it's not? Perhaps the difference relates to the more common English or American structuring. Whichever, take your pick. For what it's worth, I don't indent first lines following blank lines, whether one or two. In my last novel I added a second blank line; in this book only one was used.

Don't clutter text by overusing the likes of *however*, *moreover* and *nevertheless*.

Eliminate clutter. Zinsser's *On Writing Well*: Writing improves in direct ratio to the number of things we can keep out of it that shouldn't be there. ...the secret of good writing is to strip every sentence to its cleanest components. Every word that serves no function, every long word that could be a short word, every adverb which carries the same meaning that is already in the verb, every passive construction that leaves the reader unsure... Found in Strunk/White's *Elements of Style*: Vigorous writing is concise. A sentence should contain no unnecessary words, a paragraph no unnecessary sentences. Abridged clutter clearing examples (from->to): made up his mind -> decided, in advance of -> before, did not remember -> forgot...

Often said, even overstated, but ever true: show, don't tell. Rather than stating '...a painter,' use an example '...picked up a brush and laid a stroke on the canvass.'

Double check chapters for the clarity of continuity, in particular where chapters switch between characters, places or time periods.

At the end of a chapter add a teaser or hint of what's to come to entice the reader to read on, start the next chapter now rather than waiting until later.

Ever be on the lookout for abused or overused words, those you may use incorrectly or have a tendency to repeat in particular. We all do it! *You* or *your*? Inclined to abuse words like *something*, I seek out such culprits and fix or replace them: EDIT > FIND with a mouse or [ctrl]+[F] (hold down first, tap second key) on the computer keyboard.

Be wary of backside add-ons to words that detract from the quality of the word itself, like *ize, ness, ing* or *ingly.*

Vary sentence structure, from a straightforward statement to one shifted about 'He walked to the wall, after checking...' -> 'After checking..., he walked to the wall,' to alter rhythm and balance your material.

Continuity and sequencing: For fiction the former overshadows the latter. For non-fiction, such as this book, sequencing gains importance: what goes where, and what should be grouped with it.

To properly revise your work you need to be able to adopt the attitude of someone else. For editing you must become a critical and ruthless reader. Concentrate on each and every word and phrase as you examine what that alter ego put together. Slash away. Accept nothing that fails to measure up. Does each and every word, sentence and paragraph relate to and support the plot? Anything unneeded, trite or missing? Can what remains be further improved? Is the overall structure and layout as good as it can get, as it's going to get?

For the last manuscript pass, or even the last two, in particular, reread the dialogue aloud. Does it all still sound logical and suitable for the characters? Any doubts, set the material aside for a bit and have another go at it later. It's amazing what the passage of time does to one's perspective.

If you work on a computer, revise onscreen and, that done, attack printouts with a red pen in hand. What appears acceptable onscreen may not be so appealing on paper. Revise. Expand and trim. Add more dialogue. Attack adverbs and adjectives and keep only those truly worthy. For words that fall short, substitute better ones, in particular with verbs and nouns.

For the very last pass (perhaps using VIEW > PRINT LAYOUT to provide an altered perspective), if the content will only be self-edited (see next section), have a go and then wait a bit.

Rested, retackle the material, making sure you've changed that hat, from writer to judicious editor. That's not a switch many writers handle well, but, unless you can afford to hire a competent and recommended editor, your typescript will have to survive with nothing beyond your efforts.

A proper edit can be expensive ($70 per hour or a per-page equivalent?) but proofreading for grammar and spelling is more affordable, is better than moving ahead without some assistance. Both should be considered, in particular if written English isn't right up there among your admirable credits. Why waste all that invested creative effort only to end up with a shoddy product that could have been improved with reasonable outside help.

All done, take another look at how the book opens. Does it still work, flow properly? Or should it be revised in some way that'll improve its impact. A passing grade, then consider the ending; does that also pass muster?

Self-editing, an example: With my first novel, what was supposed to be a light edit turned into a trashing, although by hindsight that heavy-handed attack wasn't totally unwarranted. Anyway, rather than working with the resulting hodgepodge, trying to patch the original, I chose to rewrite the manuscript. The publisher wouldn't provide a re-edit without charging me and I declined to foot the bill. I tackled the editing job myself.

Not one of my brightest ideas, as it turned out; but it did proved to be an eye-opening learning experience. Sorting out the subsequent error count, I contributed a third of them (largely typos). The publisher's contribution, grammar glitches, in particular hard hyphens, was the result of a font-size reduction intended to reduce the number of book pages.

But...did I truly learn a lesson from that experience? Not really. Self-editing applied to the second novel (self-published) did yield better results, but not the improvement expected. And the third novel showed only minor advancement. In my defence, after a while what's on the page does indeed blur. That's why reading aloud is so important; it keeps the mind better focused.

A post-printing review instigated, note any errors discovered for later correction should another printing occur. After its initial purpose was fulfilled, I obtained and used the printer's proof copy to accumulate correction notes.

Recognize errors previously made and keep them in mind as something to avoid for a later project. Spelling. Grammar. Typos. One-timers or repeaters. Writers all have a bad habit or two that is best avoided.

If self-publishing, do try to trim book-creation costs by completing as much of the book interior as possible yourself. Choose and apply: margins, font choices, text justification, page sizing, headers and/or footers.

While revising, keep an eye on page layout. Scan content for problems and glitches such as unintended spaces or incorrect punctuation. Always keep an eye out for improvement: chapter continuity, sentence mix, flow, rhythm and overall appearance. Does what you see measure up to expectations?

What about chapter headings, paragraph indents, use of quotation marks (single or double?) for dialogue? And consistency? How's the spelling and grammar? Don't totally rely on what your wordprocessor advises.

Keep track of the manuscript page count if book size is a factor. Roughly how many initial manuscript pages do you want to end up with? And, how many book-sized pages will that count produce? Aside from cosmetic or other considerations, the number of pages and paper thickness affects printing and shipping costs. And if a book doesn't fit through the slot in the post office's plastic guide, postage cost escalates, can more than double for a single book.

I adopted wider margins and shifted the start of chapter text lower for my third novel. Those and a few other changes produced an unexpected increase in the number of book pages. Rather than try to change the settings or trim the book interior I asked the printer to use thinner paper. As it turned out, the thinner pages (thinnest he could print on) actually improved the feel of the book. I used the same paper thickness for this book, despite it having fewer pages than its predecessor.

Converting the book's interior to a PDF file (what a printer wants), representing a minor time factor in producing a book and is a task perhaps best left to someone else. Several programs can produce the necessary Portable Document Format file, including Adobe Acrobat, a program few writers would find other uses for.

With a bit of digging around, a print-ready book conversion can be obtained for considerably less than a hundred dollars. But first, ensure that your pre-conversion file is shipshape, fully as intended, before seeking a PDF conversion. Afterwards, any needed changes will likely have to be corrected in the source file, thus requiring another conversion. To establish what can be altered in a PDF file and what cannot, check with a conversion source or that printer you've chosen to deal with.

When considering the cover (see a subsequent section), will it match or suit the book's interior? Should you spend much time on the cover beyond providing some input regarding content and layout? Creation and providing its PDF ($200 to $500+) is a chore likely best left to someone more experienced, an individual with the required software. Many facets of that task are beyond what most writers or their gear can handle. The dollars involved and time required to acquire needed skills would likely be better invested in improving the book's interior.

For this book—a simple cover involved, one I thought suited the content—I tackled the cover myself with no more than MS Word's capabilities. I expect a publishing program would have done it better but I didn't have one. Would getting someone else to do it could have produced a better result? Maybe. I favoured a plain cover (stand out?) and wanted to see what I could accomplish. Adobe Acrobat converted the results to a PDF file. How did it turn out? Decent. Passable. Lacking. Dull. Should the layout have been more complex?

Ready to Go?

Typescript shipshape, before any conversion you'll need to remove any existing interim page numbers, headers or footers. Better still, don't number, or add a header or footer to, chapter pages at the outset. If not already as intended for the final manuscript, alter font(s) and size(s). Or, better still, adopt a font and size to be used as the default for other computer use.

Check or tidy up the final 8.5x11 inch pages for layout, paragraph indents, proper dashes and ellipses, justification, hyphenation and text positioning on page.

Within the wordprocessor try the ¶ (show/hide) icon at the top of the screen to check for errant extra spaces. If not on view, it can be added to bar by clicking on >> to the right.

Settle positioning of chapter identification (number, title) and the first line of the text on pages, and then check that such positioning is consistent throughout the manuscript.

Rerun through chapters, pursuing any missed or stray characters, any layout or content problems, anything else previously overlooked. There's no such thing as making too many passes through the material.

When you feel you've done your best, that you're finished, at least for the present, why not run the results by a writing-savvy friend, one prepared to be critical? Ask her or him to review the manuscript with a critical eye, a highlighter and/or red pen in hand for paper, seeking out what's right or wrong, overly duplicated or what needs added clarification. Request that continuity or sequencing be assessed, that weak spots be indicated. While you should not dictate or direct the scrutiny approach it's important to suggest that specific items be targeted, perhaps in particular aspects of your writing that concern you more than others.

Normally, avoid having family or friends scan your manuscript—they too often wish to be kind. Instead, get feedback from a writing group, exchange work with another writer or hire someone qualified to share the burden. Remember that enduring adage: free advice is worth the price. People trying to be helpful may actually hinder. What's needed is polite yet honest and constructive critique, solid suggestions for improvement.

If your book will include a rear page about you and previous writing achievements, that page should be printed in a smaller font size than used in the chapters or sections. And, do consider including a photo. Additionally, to be easier noted, that page should appear as a right-hand, odd numbered, page.

You may have to force that placement by adding a page break to create a blank page.

Along with checking the 'author page' placement, before accepting that all's as it should be, that it's okay to proceed with the PDF conversion (see section on this), ensure that the sought and received ISBN details, as received, plus any other pertinent data, are included on the back of the title page.

Is there a contents listing, and does it show correct book-sized page numbers? Should you make any manuscript changes after shifting to book-sized pages, check to see if or how changes made affected listing numbers—or better still, assign numbers as your final step in the process.

All that done, on to the next section for expanded comment on rewrite and revision, with some items already mentioned repeated to ensure that they're not overlooked...

Revising, Rewriting & Editing

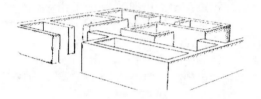

But, I use a computer and surely the wordprocessor will take care of such nitty-gritty, all those proofreading, grammar and spelling bits and pieces. Shouldn't I focus on creative issues; get that good stuff, what's been rattling around in my head, down on paper rather than fussing over petty detail?

Not so! At one point or another all that contributes to producing a decent book must be addressed, sorted and set into place. A computer program has its limits and what it suggests may not always be correct (in particular for grammar) or the best solution for the context. If you do not do your part adequately, make that extra effort to ensure that all's as it should be, that fledgling book will never have a chance of becoming a creation that reaches above, escapes, mediocrity.

That said, at the outset, grammar, spelling and structure should be ignored in favour of concentrating on committing to paper or a computer file all that great material bouncing about awaiting an opportunity to escape and be put to use. Aside from addressing glaring errors, leave that drudgery for a later day, when it will have to be dealt with, one way or another: word substitution, presentation alternatives, sentence structuring, abbreviations, punctuation. Perhaps using a few contractions. All those factors essential to bringing together a manuscript of which you can be truly proud.

But there are considerations beyond proofreading. The three words in the above section title embrace so much more, like reviewing and restructuring, expanding or condensing, correcting and polishing to name but a few.

No matter how good you feel about your creation at any point in the process, don't become complaisant. Keep focused. Rewrite and then rewrite some more. Find richer words; nouns or verbs that'll stand alone, without being artificially propped up with trite adjectives or adverbs. Avoid weak words, like interesting or pretty; captivating or gorgeous sound so much better and are more descriptive.

Some of what appears in the previous manuscript sections is intentionally repeated here. For good reason. Several items warrant mentioning again, to ensure that they are not overlooked. Revision and rewriting is in fact no more than an extension of what should have been accomplished during the process of getting it all down on paper.

While attending to all that must be done, ever remember that consistent backup is critical, should be an adhered to routine, preferably to multiple media. Make a change; backup the file. Better safe than sorry.

I first intended to divide this section into portions that separated revision and rewrite from editing, since the latter could also involve someone beyond the author working on the material. That approach became progressively more difficult to adopt and follow as the first two logically dip or flow into editing. They are all part and parcel of the nitty-gritty aspects of that essential tidy-up task.

Having already bought a few of them, do read and refer to the likes of Strunk and White's *Elements of Style,* Zinsser's *On Writing Well* or Fowler's *Modern English Usage* for particular assistance. Also worthy: Michael Moore's *A Writer's Handbook of Current English* (Canadian), *The Canadian Style* (Secretary of State), *The Canadian Writer's Guide* (Canadian Authors Association). Or perhaps consider *The Modern Writer's Handbook* (US, Frank O'Hare and Edward A. Kline). Check library shelves and larger books stores for other helpmates that, subsequent to scrutiny, still appear worthy.

In secondary school my success in French exceeded accomplishments in English. That's not to say that what I achieved in either was all that commendable. But, over the years due to lack of use, the French capability declined. Written English improved, largely as a result of repeated application, writing projects and feedback received or reactions noted. Business letters. Systems procedures. Computer-related articles. Travel-oriented pieces. Essays. Tackling a first book, and then another. Each and every attempt to add words to pages hopefully improved an ability to do so, as did ever being an avid reader. For me, through the years revision time invested has always exceeded the hours initially devoted to creating material.

Some Nitty Gitty

Check what you've written for an excessive number of characters or disproportionate narrative. Don't confuse or bore that all-important reader.

Ensure that valueless interjection doesn't impede the plot flow.

Review dialogue and ever seek to improve it.

Trim or expand the material. Replace or eliminate trite or laboured portions.

Always keep an eye out for awkward phrasing, spelling errors, typos and punctuation flaws, aside from the intervention of computer spelling and grammar checking.

Do chapters end where they should? Does the closing sentence entice a reader to turn the page and read on?

Does your story shift between characters, scenes or time periods? If so, some kind of transitional phrasing may be needed. Are those you've chosen the best ones? For each such change you need to let the reader know what you are doing, where you are going. Add a word or phrase to indicate a shift. For example: 'Later...,' 'Back at the...,' 'Meanwhile...,' 'While that was going on...' Or, to indicate that one paragraph clearly relates to another, repeat a word from the previous sentence or paragraph to tie things together: '...tall ships. These unique ships...'

A blank line or two between paragraphs helps indicate a more significant change. Or add centered asterisks (***) with a blank line before and after for added distinction, to indicate a more extreme or important time or setting shift, perhaps flashback.

Bear in mind that constantly working on the same material can and likely will breed diminishing returns. At some point what's on a page will blur and become meaningless. That's the time to set it aside and tackle something else. Returning to the material later should add a fresher perspective.

Run the material by someone with a helpful inclination and a measure of writing skill. Hopefully (s)he will contribute a differing viewpoint, suggest considerations that never entered your mind or failed to remain long enough to register. Structural irregularities. Insufficient conflict. A shaky premise. Too predictable a plotline. Deficient dialogue.

Does your tale have logical continuity? Is the sequencing of events credible?

Does each and every word suit the setting or characters?

Are your characters consistent and plausible?

Is your diction appropriate? The proper choice and use of words and phrases adds flavour to a story. It may formally employ English conventions or be used more informally to suit the tale, its characters or locale. Why not put to good use colloquialisms, dialect/idiom or jargon (lawyers, accountants, engineers, doctors, scientists).

How about syntax, dealing with how words are assembled?

And, style? Add some personal flavour to how words and phrases are gathered together.

What could be deleted without loss of flow or content? De-clutter. Trim the underbrush. Cull out deadwood. Ensure that nothing superfluous or digressing hinders the tale's proper advancement. Something debatable encountered, will removing it detract from or improve storyline delivery?

Have you found a need for or made use of an ellipsis (...) or a long or short dash? If so, did you use either properly? If not, check that grammar source you should have nearby. Both serve a purpose and can be used to enhance the presentation of what you are writing.

Watch for words duplicated too close together, those not intended for effect.

Ensure that pronouns used (she, he) properly relate to the character last mentioned by name or direct reference.

Where appropriate, convert negative phrasing into positive or something less negative: '...is not to be denied.' -> '...is to be recognised or accepted.' '...is not wanted.' -> '...is unwanted.'

Although rewrite, re-working existing text, is a close cousin to editing it's not necessarily one and the same. Motivation and mindset differ, or they should. Rewriting is or applies to the earlier ongoing effort, an undertaking that focuses on adding to, deleting from or reshaping portions of material. Editing is more a project-completing re-assessment of content, by you or someone else.

Should you decide—foolishly, as I discovered earlier on—that you are up to that wrapping-up editing task, or feel that your book or article budget can't accommodate a hefty edit bill, march forward with caution. Try to be objective and be prepared for the time where you will hate the sight of what you've written. As the task unfolds, it will appear a seemingly endless battle: review and change, re-scan and alter some more, delete or substitute.

Before tackling the editor role, set the work aside for a while. Free your mind and try to distance yourself from the material. Do something else. Then address the chore as if it was someone else tackling those assembled words. Be brutal! Challenge each and every word, sentence, paragraph or chapter. Make sure that one sentence or paragraph properly flows into the next and suitably contributes its fair share.

Do you have a willing and savvy friend prepared to be ruthless if need be? Curious about my success in self-editing, I had a friend who gets a big kick from having a go at what I write scan one of my novels—after printing, unfortunately. His assessment proved rather embarrassing. Most mistakes discovered were typos or they resulted from incomplete sentence revision: fix one portion and miss doing what was needed to another. Nonetheless, the number of mishaps surprised me, having gone through the text six or so times.

Beyond dealing with grammar, word choices and the proper use of sentences and paragraphs, at some point page mechanics must be assessed or re-assessed—before or after shifting from manuscript-sized pages what's chosen as a book size: page layout and justification, margins, hyphenation, headers or footers.

That Final Edit Run

Since few realistic writers fully edit their own work or do it well, dedicated editors manage to make a decent or lucrative living. Even those less talented manage to prosper. For an author not lucky enough to land a traditional publisher (most costs covered), a comprehensive edit represents a substantial potential expenditure, one often proving prohibitive. But, a piece of work lacking a decent edit may no measure up.

What to do? Shelve the effort, put to waste all that work? Live with a shoddy result?

Writers who cannot afford to hire an editor have little choice unless they have a willing friend with the appropriate skills. They may have to settle for self-editing. While editing what others write may not be easy, spotting errors in your writing ranges from difficult to impossible, despite making that writer-to-editor mindset shift attempt. The eye too easily passes over errors that others will without doubt notice.

Before tackling the job on your own, acquire a couple specific how-to books on the subject (see list in last book section). Read them cover-to-cover and then do it again with a highlighter in hand. Make notes of what's most important, and re-review what you've marked during the self-editing chore. Go through the manuscript as many times as it takes to become satisfied with the results.

Editing demands a critical eye. Beyond proofreading, an editor normally reorganises the work, to one extent or another. (S)he ensures that the opening and closing make sense and that what's in between logically flows from sentence to sentence, from paragraph to paragraph and chapter to chapter. An editor assesses the main plot and any sub-plots, characters, settings and a host of other aspects that contribute to a polished manuscript. (S)he scans narrative and substitutes engaging dialogue where needed—or the reverse if that's the better choice.

Something completed in hand, you might not be done yet. For an article or book, to suit publication requirements, a word or page count may have to be met. Material may have to be added or lesser-contributing portions may have to be trimmed, without obscuring or losing the essence of the material.

Nowadays most readers don't appreciate, may even object to, excessive narrative. Faced with lumps of it they may decide to move on and read something else. Dialogue must be good, even better than good. It's crucial and it's what publishers and readers want. To survive, a firm's books must sell well, and in volume. To accomplish that publishers cater to the whims of the buying public, those folk with funds to spend on books.

No matter how much time you spend rehashing what's written, go over dialogue once again. Is there enough of it? Does it sound real, like what someone might actually say?

Explanations attached to dialogue should be minimized. Beef up the dialogue content to cover and deliver what's needed. Scrutinise attributes (he said, she uttered). Are they all needed? Any used too often? Properly structured dialogue should require few to properly identify the speaker.

Add appropriate beats (action bits like He *mopped his brow.*) to support or emphasise what's being said.

Back in DOS Days (pre-Windows), from the mid-1980s and into the early 1990s, I worked with a DOS version of *WordStar*, the most popular computer-based writing tool back then. While I eventually recognised and admitted its shortcomings, abandoned it, for many years it was a trusted helpmate, a program used both for creating documents and computer programming.

To that wordprocessor used to produce the manuscript for my first book that got published, I'd added a pop-up thesaurus: cursor on a word, a keystroke combination invoked the utility and up popped a list of substitute words. As I recall its capability, that thesaurus surpassed what's currently built into MS Word.

Neither, however, could or can replace a hefty book-form thesaurus I always keep close to hand, ever aware that provided synonyms aren't always equal or correct for a particular context. Unsure of the meaning of a potential substitute word, check it out in that dictionary that also should be within reach.

As boring as it may seem to some writers, spending time with a dictionary is well worthwhile. I have a friend addicted to doing just that. He relishes sharing his discoveries with me. Ideal for casual browsing, why not take a smaller version along on a bus to help pass the time.

While our numbers are dwindling, writers familiar with what some consider the good old DOS (pre-Windows) days may recall evaluation programs such as *RightWriter* (favoured style) and *Grammatik* (leaned more toward grammar). Just like what's built into MS Word, what they disclosed couldn't always be accepted as gospel. As helpful as such utilities were or may yet be, they're fallible. Never assume what's reported as being correct. Just as is MS Word, they're structured upon a grammar-rules database and what's advised may or may not accurately accommodate differing context. Despite it acting a bit quirky within Windows XP and unlikely to survive another operating system upgrade, I still occasionally use *RightWriter*—on a floppy disk, double-clicking on the program file to fire it up.

Acceptability aside, suggestions made by such utilities should at least nudge a writer into reconsidering the words or phrasing chosen. The same attention should be applied to those squiggly green lines added by MS Word as a flag to indicate what it perceives to be a grammatical error. I never ignore them. After pausing to review the objection indicator and decide if it's correct or not for the context, on occasion I rewrite the phrase just to get rid of the marker.

In DOS days I discovered other handy-dandy freebie helpmates on computer bulletin boards (precursor to the internet). *Fogfinder* assessed text and presented a graph that slotted the work according to popular magazines, ranging from the Atlantic Monthly to Readers' Digest. *Wordfreq* counted word usage for a document and presented a list of its findings. As I upgraded to newer versions of Windows, I lost them one by one but have yet to seek any replacements via the internet.

Of the lot, my favourite was *PC-Style*, a utility that still functions. Kept on a floppy disk—like *RightWriter*, with that trusty old *WordStar* version no longer in use—it only accepts straight-text files. Rapidly producing a neat little graph assessing readability, its judgement is based upon a preference for short sentences, personal tone and action words.

Don't Be Dull

Want to avoid being considered an amateur? Sure you do. Everyone does. Pep up flat writing. Put a little zing into it. Add a few contractions (it's...). Why say walk when you could say trudge, stroll, rove, ramble, range or saunter? Avoid worn out words like 'interesting.' Substitute better, more descriptive, words.

Don't repeat yourself, unless intended for effect. Zero in on overused words and replace them. For example, abusing words like *something, need* or *while,* I find I routinely scan chapters or sections and replace them. Assuming you are using MS Word or another wordprocessor with a similar feature, use EDIT > FIND—or [Ctrl]+[F] on the keyboard (hold first key down and tap the second)—to unearth overused words or phrases, other items requiring corrective consideration. It's also handy for finding an adjacent known word to get to something difficult to spot within a sea of text. If a multiple same-word quest, work your way through the document by tapping the [Enter] key.

Years ago I recognised that many words were superior to, more interesting than, others and started listing those I liked. While a good idea at the outset, I ended up with a bulging list that, still around somewhere, I soon declined to consult. To mentions a few: naysayer, blatant, austere, capitulation, blather, gimcrack, dross, spurious, curmudgeon, maelstrom, posthaste. Unfortunately I've managed to use few of them, aside from those that appear in opening some sections of this book.

Improve the verbs and nouns you use. Rather than say laugh, use chuckle, chortle, cackle, snicker or titter. Instead of nonsense, try bunkum, claptrap, balderdash, poppycock or flapdoodle.

If in doubt as to how to correct a debatable word, sentence or paragraph, mark it for later consideration. Add a few blank lines ahead of it or add asterisks (****) before and after a word or use a few arrows (>>>>, <<<<).

A word about clichés. While some purists despise and won't use them, I find the odd one admirably addresses a particular situation: as is or adapted to avoid the controversial use of such worn-out phrases. An intriguing website: westegg.com/cliché.

Which to use: its or it's, compare/agree with or to, as or like, can or may, whom or who, that or which, number or quantity, less or fewer? To clarify these and others, consult a decent grammar tome or one of the books listed in the last section.

Who or whom ever plagues me. While I know that *whom* applies to the object of an action and *who* refers to the one taking the action, what's proper for a particular context isn't always clear, at least to me. I must admit that, given the dilemma, I often chicken out and just rewrite the sentence. Not admirable but...

Use commas as and where needed, grammatically or to indicate a needed pause within a sentence. But do so sparingly. If in doubt don't add one, provided the sentence still reads properly, is fully understandable. There are grammar conventions, and exceptions that may be tolerated. I recall a secretary who once worked for me. She disputed my use of commas but guess who won most often (or preferred to think so), despite the possible validity of what she might have wanted to use.

Multiple adjectives are supposed to have a comma between them. Well, I don't always do that, depending upon how it reads without one. And what about the periods between U and after S or at the end of Mr. In books I've seen periods used and not. For novels, and some other projects, where I feel I can get away with it, I favour leaving the periods out, whether totally correct or not. The simpler the better...

What's truly important is to spice up the writing for those essential readers. They want to see, hear, touch, smell or taste what's on a page. Show, don't tell. Use comparisons. Display emotions within dialogue. As a character name, try an adaptation; I recall once seeing a person identified as Dickless Tracy. Plays on words are currently the *in* thing, although some uses are less clever than others. An article I wrote about digital cameras was entitled (not by me) 'Pixel this...' What about something like *ant-hole*; sounds better than what it suggests to some.

Write about what you know or can imagine in sufficient detail to make the material sound plausible. Avoid shoddy speculation that'll come back to haunt you.

Watch for unmatched nouns and verbs where singular should be plural or vice versa. 'That pair appears...' 'None of us likes...' 'Data are...' 'The pack surges ahead.' 'Members of the club demand...' 'The department is...' 'Those in the department are...'

Join a Writing Group

Perhaps a group of like-minded individuals could prove helpful, would offer helpful critiquing feedback? But not everyone can accept constructive criticism. Not sure why that is, but the two writing groups I belong to have been great, both for screening portions of a novel in progress and for vetting articles headed for a seniors-oriented newspaper column.

No such group handy? Start one, it's not difficult. Check the internet for critiquing guidelines.

For such a group to be effective, it should consist of writers roughly at the same capability level. A novice mixed in with others considerably more experienced can prove disruptive or can tend to shift sessions to the lower denominator. While some may accept or tolerate that, others may soon move on to another group to obtain what they seek, what they first arrived in search of.

Critiquing is not criticising, although 'constructive criticism' fits the bill since the intent is to provide helpful comment and suggestions. Material read aloud, as an opening gesture why not begin your critiquing contribution with a positive/encouraging word or two about what you heard. Follow that with objective/specific/concise comment on what you didn't understand or what you thought failed to complement the material.

Remarks already made by other listeners shouldn't be repeated, except perhaps to reinforce an important suggestion that appeared to have been ignored or undervalued by the reader.

Readers, aside from any introduction, should listen after reading, not speak. They must understand that attacking their writing isn't the intent. At the outset they may choose to state what comment in particular is sought. After that, they shouldn't respond to individual critiquing except to answer a specific question.

Comments received, the reader must then decide which to accept and what to ignore or discard. After all, the writing belongs to the writer and (s)he has the final say on what'll appear in her or his work.

Some items for listeners to consider:

- If not a segment of something larger does the beginning grab your interest?
- Does the ending tie it all together?
- Two or more stories bundled together in the one piece, is the material confusing?
- Does content contribute to the plot, move the story forward?
- Is the action plot-directed, focused, rather than merely tossed in?
- Is there sufficient dialogue and does it all work?
- Are speakers clearly defined?
- Are dialogue attributes/tags overdone or underdone (s/he said...)?
- Are there too many characters?
- Are characters clearly distinguishable?
- Are character/setting descriptions suitable; excessive or too brief?
- At times is there more explanation than a reader wants or needs to know?
- Is the point of view consistent, with any departures appropriate?

- Are comparisons, metaphors or similes used to advantage?
- Are clichés overdone?
- Any useless words begging to be removed?
- Is use of passive voice (is, was...) excessive?
- Are sentence lengths too long, too short or well mixed?
- Are all adjectives and adverbs needed?
- Are nouns or verbs the best available?
- Is the tense consistently, with any departures appropriate?

And Now What?

Don't become discouraged. No matter how much you write, how many articles or books are completed, only a portion of your efforts will ever be rewarded. Over the years I've contributed articles to two newspaper columns and a variety of other publications. Some efforts produced income, other didn't. Of articles written, half got published. Of those published, I got paid for half. Some were bartered, exchanged for value. Within the half that generated income, half again paid decently or better. My books are subsidised by article income.

My most lucrative writing venture involved supplying computer sections for an accounting text— that paid extremely well. That aside, I'm not deterred. I press onward.

With three middling+ novels and this book behind me, I await further input for a non-fiction farming piece and I'll next tackle a travel anthology that will bring together related articles written over the years, both those published and not. Adapting those to book content, personal aspects and thoughts, originally removed to accommodate travel publication requirements at the time, will be re-introduced.

Well the manuscript's now done...or is it? Perhaps another swing through is needed to ensure that each and every word, sentence or paragraph is as and where it should be, that the layout and fonts are as intended, that all's neat and tidy. If I'd not been so tired of going through my third novel, so intent on wrapping it up, I'd have noticed that the font size used for the author page at the back of the book was too larger. Ah well, can't win them all, or so *they* say.

After completing and rewriting sections 3, 4, 5 and 6 I worried that some items were mentioned too many times or were not grouped with related comment, where they should be or in the proper section within the four. Another reason for that extra run through...

A Revision Checklist

Does:

- each word, sentence and paragraph add value, enhance the material?
- each chapter ending induce a reader to start the next one?
- the material mesh, move toward as originally intended?
- your creation's opening provide impact?
- the book's closing wrap up the plot, leave few or no loose ends?
- the material have the right balance of narrative and great dialogue?

- the text reflect a measure of personal flavour?
- the work provide a flow that's logical, one that will appeal to readers?
- your creation contain any obscure portions that need clarifying?
- the material omit wimpy adjectives and adverbs, utilise better nouns and verbs?
- your effort contain too many words that may not be understood?
- the work avoid passive voice, employ active?
- the text remain in the proper tense, with appropriate departures?
- the material retain overlooked repetition?
- your creation contain any lingering grammatical or spelling errors?
- the text, having been read aloud, reflect attempts to improve it?

Interior completed at long last, it's now time to move on to other aspects of what's required to properly wrap up the project: a cover to design, a package to be structured in a fashion favourable to readers and acceptable to a printer. And then there's all that must be done after printing: dispose of printed copies, keep track of book traffic and earnings...

The Cover

While it may offend some authors—those enamoured with their creation—the truth of the matter has been time-tested and proven to be true. Covers count! Most writing gurus agree that good cover design is vital and that it will attract readers, those so important potential book buyers. In particular for fiction, first impressions are crucial. The competition to capture book buyers is fierce.

According to those in the know a potential buyer spends mere seconds looking at a front cover. If intrigued, perhaps double that time scanning the back cover to find out what the book's all about. If they like what they see, they may then peek inside and after that might even buy the book.

That a book's spine is normally what's exposed in a library or on a bookshop's shelf is no reason to ignore cover potential. Readers shopping for entertainment do extract books from a shelf and an attention-grabbing cover may just persuade a reader to dig out the cash or the plastic.

On a scale of one to ten, how would you rate the value of book covers you've browsed? Did any particular wrapping encourage you to seriously consider venturing inside, perhaps completing the transaction? If so, why? On the front: graphics, fonts, colours or the combination. On the back: pictures, endorsements, a contents briefing or the price. Was the ensemble fresh, unusual or different for some reason? What about colour choices?

Accepting that a cover is so important, for your book, do invest the time. Carefully choose what will be wrapped around the material that consumed all that effort and concentration. Think like a reader, which I assume you are anyway, to whatever extent. Scan covers found in libraries and bookshops. Note content, colour combinations, layout and any unusual treatments. Whatever the discoveries, ensure that what you end up with will seize a roving eye and that it somehow relates to the book's content.

Hard covers were once plentiful but cost for the producer and resulting pricing for buyers have reduced their popularity. Or perhaps the added weight alienated readers who prefer to sit back and balance what they're reading in one hand. Nowadays, perfect-bound (spine glued) soft covers, larger than pocket books, are more the norm, in particular for novels. What I adopted is a popular size: 5.5 x 8.5 inches. Pocket books, long rather consistent in dimension, appear to be lengthening.

For the first of my three published novels (all perfect bound) I had little say in the cover design. The graphic I suggested and provided wasn't used. The publisher's choice wasn't objectionable, was actually rather appealing. But it wasn't really accurate. The book's content was largely set in Greece and the head that appeared on the cover was Roman, complete with a laurel wreath.

The cover for the second novel was derived from what I discovered in a couple pieces of clipart. Magnified via a spotlight extraction of a spot within mountainous territory, it depicted someone climbing a rock face. While what I provided might not have won any prizes, the cover did at least relate to the book content. Suggestions from the printer altered my colour choice and shadings.

The cover and spine design (above) for a third novel—combining limited experience and added deliberation—was all mine, for better or worse. Background: blue shadings, white title lettering, black text elsewhere. The coloured picture: a melding of a koala and an Asian street scene—both components of the storyline.

Using black lettering on a blue spine was a debatable choice. White would have stood out more (better catch a reader's roving eye?) but then black being harder to read may cause a reader to pull out the book to check the cover. Who knows, eh? The printer did the composition and created the PDF-file for that cover.

While both covers reflected what could be found inside the wrapping, the image for *No More Illusions,* more a sketch than a picture, wasn't as well received as the cover that followed, the one for *Coming Up Short.* In general, that later cover was more like others to be found on bookshelves. Nonetheless I liked the former one, for what that's worth. One bookshop manager, after turning that book about in his hands, outright rejected *No More Illusions.* He didn't like the appearance or 'feel' of, self-published books. That was said without at all considering the interior content. Would he have reacted to the later book, that cover being more in keeping with others to be found on his shelves? Based upon the previous reception, I didn't return...

In developing a concept for a cover, do bear in mind that it's difficult to be different—defy convention, what's more commonly found, with impunity. To achieve a successful result in terms of book saleability, unless the departure is something sensational and acceptable to the buying public, keeping within the bounds of the pack is likely the better path to follow.

From the back cover of *Coming Up Short*: 'Steve Wrift, an accountant fated to attract trouble, is fired from a job and abandons Canada's West Coast for employment in Australia. With travel time to spare, he arranges a stopover in Japan to visit a penpal. Visiting Kamakura he's given a piece of jade by a member of the yakuza, Japan's version of the mafia. That stone later discarded in frustration, Steve discovers another on a bed pillow after a night of passion in Hong Kong. A lonely Steve, settled in Melbourne, must deal with a vengeful female boss. While debating limited options, he bumps into a reformed Charlie Tucker, a wastrel friend from the past with whom Steve has shared mishaps, on and off since they first met in Istanbul. Checking into a company problem in Sydney, Steve discovers more than expected. Meanwhile, Charlie wrestles with complications arising from a personal relationship.'

Completing the back cover: the price ($17.00) and a barcode.

Overall, decent? Appealing to readers? Could the cover components be improved? One item or more? If so, how? Reconsidering it now, perhaps I'd tweak this or that, but, in total, I remain satisfied with it.

The cover of the first novel (*Shattered Expectations*) was laminated and it curled somewhat. Neither of the two books that followed had coated covers. Yet they weren't drab. Colour applications?

Since this book's wrapping is rather plain, even a tad dull, I thought it needed something extra, that lamination might just dress it up some. The coating issue unsettled at this pre-printing point in the process, how did the cover turn out?

Considering how you value the content, doesn't it deserve a painstakingly developed wrapping, warrant the best achievable? Layout and content. Picture or sketch. Title and positioning. Font selections and sizes. Colours and shadings. Managing all that can prove a daunting task for most writers, one beyond selection and assembly skills, something unachievable with installed software.

That's why cover designers get to charge all those big bucks. In designing your cover, would you expect a designer to read the book? How many would actually do that? Few I expect. That's why the onus is on you to suggest and decide what may or may be suitable.

You can't judge a book by its cover, or so some say. Despite that old saw, that's what people frequently do. Bear that in mind and invest the time and effort, in good measure.

The Title

How important is the title, as part of the cover package? Consider your last trip to a bookshop. Did any titles jump out and grab your attention? If so, why? For which books read in the past do you recall the titles? Again, why? How about *To Kill A Mockingbird*, *Catch-22* (that's become a commonly used phrase), *Lust For Life*, *Lie Down In Darkness*, *For Whom The Bell Tolls* and *The Catcher In The Rye*? What's appealing about those titles and why are any of them memorable?

Put on your thinking cap and return to the issue throughout the project. Don't rest until you've come up and settled upon something unique, a title that'll distinguish your labour of love from all the others crowding those bookshop shelves you have an eye on. Got one? Let the matter rest for a bit. Returning to it, does the title still provide the same tingle, an enduring sense of achievement and satisfaction?

For my three novels (same two main characters but self-standing tales) the titles all relate to the key character in the book, reflect how that accountant manages to lose or degrade what he started out his business life with: *Shattered Expectations, No More Illusions, Coming Up Short.* Each title suggests or implies a sense of confronting reality and failing to measure up. They represent an accumulation of confrontations and disappointments. Good choices? The best? If not, why not?

For an upcoming non-fiction book about years on a local farm I listed some twenty potential names, each containing the same key word. I finally chose one but expect that once the project is underway I'll return to that listing to revisit that initial choice.

Limit the title to three or four words, more only if truly needed and the title works. Try to have it reflect the theme or a key element of what's inside. Run the chosen title by a friend or two—acceptance or rejection, their thoughts, suggestions, reasoning?

For example, I just read an engaging book, one with a short title appropriate to content: *Water Inc*, a first novel by Varda Burstyn. Well crafted, it chronicles an attempt by corporate America to extract water from Quebec to feed thirsty states below the border. A good read. A believable premise, with tension included to hold attention and moves the tale along.

As already mentioned, most books in a shop are placed on the shelf spine out and upright. Yet, most titles and author names run with the length of a spine. Potential buyers must tilt their head to decipher the letters—not the best way to catch the eye of a prospective buyer, in particular if the volume is slim, as is this one.

For this book I used vertical lettering, for two reasons. One: easier to read with the book in an upright position. Two: I could do the spine lettering with little difficulty within the wordprocessor I use. Not sure how that turned out, abbreviated as needed for a fit. What do you think? Would you have done it differently? If so, how?

Just having the spine on view isn't much to work with but hopefully it will induce a reader to extract the book and inspect the cover. Maybe this book's condensed title, aside from the 'Writing' part, will pique curiosity. Or not. Lucky are the authors who manage to get their book positioned on a shelf with the cover fully displayed. Even luckier are those who find their books displayed in a window or set out atop the shop's counter.

Shelf competition is fierce. If you want your book to flourish amidst the masses, do your bit in creating the cover. Ponder what's needed. Don't be shy; indicate what you'd like to see. It's your book. Provide ideas that reflect a book's content or those that you can relate to the undertaking.

And, it's not just customers who may be influenced by a book's wrapping. A well-designed cover may encourage a review. Or it could get your treasure into a bookshop or library. It might assist in getting an edition re-issuing publishing contract or open other doors of opportunity.

Although there are no fixed rules when it comes to cover design, there are some generally accepted positioning guidelines. Title printed large and in the upper half of the cover. Artwork mid-cover. Author identification usually in smaller lettering toward the bottom, if you become famous the font sizing and positioning for title and author may become reversed.

For the spine, book front cover facing up, left to right: title, author and publisher's name in full or partial according to space availability.

On the back cover (top to bottom), some or all, according to space availability: synopsis of content, a picture, reviewer or promotional remarks, price, barcode. Adding a barcode on the back cover will add some $30 to the cover cost but bookshops want it, with the book price adjacent.

For all three components (cover, spine, back), keep the content simple, limiting the number of fonts used to two, perhaps three. Resist the temptation to dispose of unused space. Integrate all the components into something pleasing to the eye. Too often the back cover and spine aren't used to advantage, as limited as options may initially appear.

The back cover provides an opportunity to offer a prospective buyer a taste of what's inside. The spine has a lesser role, but the overall packaging will hopefully encourage a browser to peek inside, even come up with the purchase price.

Colour

In developing your book cover and spine, devote considerable thought to assessing the value of colour and how to use it to advantage. What choices will best entice a potential buyer to extract your book from that army of spines on a shelf? Get her or him to browse the back cover. Open the book and read a portion of the first page within. Then, perhaps, flip a few pages and sample the content.

Colour complement selected, wait a bit and then re-evaluate your choices. Do they still measure up, represent the best choice for what's inside the book? Will they appeal to the intended audience? Have you considered which hues and shadings best stimulate, excite or depress, sooth, create a feeling of warmth or foster opposing impressions?

One book's content may clamour for brighter colours, even garish, or mixed to suit. The interior of another may call for a totally different colour complement, something subdued and relaxing to the eye.

Reds stimulate the senses, may even elevate blood pressure. Blues tend to induce a calming effect. High arousal yellows, oranges and reds suggest sun, heat or fire.

Alternately, low arousal blues and greens lean more toward coolness or tranquility. Yet a brilliant turquoise may in some way stimulate a browser.

The colours you select for your book cover can enhance impact and shadings may modify that effect. The intent is to catch the eye and draw readers into the cover's imagery, and thus into the book's interior.

But colour alone won't prop up a weak cover design. It's merely one component, a segment hopefully contributing to the success of the product. What will work best for your creation, your package? Decision reached, do you later remain satisfied and sure about it, or is more deliberation needed?

For my second novel, I selected colours for the cover. Don't remember my reasoning but the printer persuaded me otherwise and his choice prevailed.

For the following book my colour choice and shadings remained unchanged. Live and learn?

Pricing?

How to decide: Pick a figure? Base it on the anticipated unit cost? Not likely! Perhaps an educated guess at what the marketplace will bear should be the pricing guide. Check bookshelves for similar books. That done, how should the average price be adjusted for how your book differs from those? Thickness? Cover differences? Your first book? But will altering the price by a dollar or two make any difference in sales? Lower maybe, but higher may not be to your advantage.

Be realistic.

If you truly feel that dropping the price a dollar or two will sell more books, do it. On the other hand, if you plan to use the book as a promotional giveaway a higher price may prove more impressive. In any case, without a rave review or two, for an unknown author, pricing a novel over twenty dollars is suspect.

In pricing books, publishers tend to add a .95 or .99 to the dollar figure. What will those inclined toward the latter do if or when pennies vanish? As I understand it, it costs more to produce a penny than it's worth today. Anyway, such book pricing reminds me of what I find so annoying at gas station pumps. But I guess it works, or they wouldn't do it. The same thing could be said of realtors and their pricing habits, but when the time comes to sell our house I expect I'll join that crowd. A price of $399,900 does sound or appear to be less than $400,000.

Why not just set a book price in whole dollars? My 1996 novel was priced at $12.95, the 2005 one, without debating the issue, was $17.95. The book published a year later I priced at $17, a figure to which the printer added a decimal point and a couple zeros. Perhaps I gave up a dollar on the last one but somehow I felt better for the simplification. And, I could have priced it at $18.

On the back of this book: $19 (no decimal point or zeros). Not a recommendation, but rounding off prices appeals to me, but then I have an accounting background, not one in cover design or book marketing. The price for this book was higher than previous books (but still under $20), despite the fewer number of pages, because it is non-fiction, a how-to guide, a book hopefully offering helpful, constructive, benefit.

Whatever the final cover price, be prepared to concede a couple dollars for a cash sale to acquaintances or at a craft sale. The net dollars received will still exceed by far what you'd get after discounting for a bookshop or a distributor.

Laminate the cover or not? Adding a plastic coating will make the cover stand up better, reduce wear and tear, but it may encourage the cover to curl. Ask about that tendency, one that may no longer be the problem that arose for my first book. That discouraged me from using the coating for following books, and I actually found that I preferred the appearance of the cover without.

Moreover, how many novels warrant added endurance? Few, I'd say. Some non-fiction efforts perhaps. Signs of wear and tear could be beneficial. Would a worn cover suggest that what's inside has been browsed frequently; suggest that the content warrants exploration? Discuss the matter with an intended publisher or printer.

Getting the Job Done

If self-publishing, save some dollars by doing whatever you can yourself. But, do recognise all that's involved. If a portion of what must be done appears beyond your capability or inclination give serious thought to employing the talents of a professional cover designer.

An experienced designer will add creativity, a fresh, uninvolved, perspective. (S)he will know how best to organise the cover's assorted requirements. Overall layout. Graphics. Colours. Text sizing and positioning. Spacing. Graphics design is more than just decoration. Properly combined, the elements of good design yield harmony and entice the roving eye.

Assuming that the selected cover designer has successfully done several covers before, (s)he should provide a range of helpful suggestions that could include related pre-press book considerations. As an added bonus, using a designer enables a writer to avoid niggling but necessary details beyond her or his interest. But...all at a price!

A designer may suggest that the inside face of the cover be utilized: inside the front for some kind of promotional text, inside the back for a picture and author outline. I don't know how much that would add to the cost of printing but I expect that adding a page or two instead would prove less expensive.

If you decide to go with a cover designer, check out other book covers. Before the first cover meeting invest an hour or two to determine what you want included or excluded in the wrapping, perhaps how you think it all should be assembled. Arrive with lots of questions. Probe for the reasoning behind what's proposed, what the designer wishes to do. Why...? why...?

Don't be overly swayed by personal taste. Keep in mind those anticipated readers, folk beyond family and friends. If seeking independent advice, focus on people who represent your target group or those who've already experienced what you are going through, are trying to sort out.

For a professional cover-design job, the cost (design plus PDF file) could run from $200 to $600 or more, depending upon who's charging, the colour range and other factors involved (eg embossing, cutouts, double front cover).

Shop around. Seek recommendations. Ask questions. References? Talk to several possible designers and request samples of previous creations. Get at least three quotes. Doubts lingering, explore provided references for the best two, bearing in mind that you're unlikely to receive any unfavourable reference names.

Being an art form, something not fully understood by many writers, some designers charge excessive dollars and still manage to attract business. Others deliver a comparable product but are more reasonable in pricing their efforts. Don't expect bargain prices but do anticipate getting value for the cost involved: access to solid and robust ideas, discussion, an overall innovative design and successful technical implementation.

Test your efforts, or those of a professional cover designer. Move back a couple metres and consider the image, in the light of what you were expecting.

Does it deliver? A successful cover should all but sparkle and beckon. It must be clearly visible, needs to create a desire for a closer look and encourage any inclination to handle the book.

Will the cover catch that often-elusive roving eye? In a shop, will it compete successfully with adjacent books? Does anything set your gem apart from others?

Novels and other fictional products differ from reference books, such as computer manuals or training material guides. Each requires a focused approach and execution. Are there any packaging conventions to be followed? Check similar books to see if there's anything not yet considered: contents listing, subscript on pages for referencing, a resource section at the back of the book, acknowledgement of the written or pictorial work of others, items introduced for clarification or as authority.

A savvy reader, after browsing the covers of similar books and reading what appears on the back, may take a peek inside. Will your package be as good as, or better than, those adjacent? Early in the game, do your research and seek a winning combination. Try to link up with someone who has already produced something similar to what you have in mind. Always ask questions, even those that seem dumb— there's no such thing. Why this...why that.

Gathering information and accumulating knowledge cannot go amiss. What's gained through research, that investment of time and energy, can only enhance your decision-making and ultimately improve what that produces.

One Perspective

For my last two books, as mentioned, I provided the cover content: overall concept and layout, artwork, fonts and sizes. A sans serif font was used for title, publisher and author name, cover and spine. On the back, a serif font, as found inside the book: Bookman Old Style. As used for this book, it's my default font for general computer document use.

For the two previous books, the printer created the PDF cover file; I provided the PDF cover file for this book, it being simpler, with no colours involved.

While the cover for my second novel may have lacked 'that professional look,' I liked it...still do. Moreover, my book budget didn't have room for a hefty cover-design outlay. The cover for the third novel was more conventional and had the benefit of previous experience.

For my last two books and this one, after some digging about, I tracked down a suitable printer, one who also did covers. The firm provided design work at a lesser cost than if I'd worked with an independent cover designer. Whether or not the results ended up equivalent to what I'd get for a larger payout to a dedicated cover designer didn't matter to me. Satisfied with the result, I appreciated not having to coordinate a designer's contribution with a printer's expectations. One-stop shopping!

For this book I invested extra time and effort debating cover content and structure. Too simple? Truly a 'book in a plain brown wrapper'? Perhaps, but I wanted the cover for this book to be different, more subdued and in keeping with its non-fiction content. I first intended black print for the cover, then decided that a darker brown (not too dark) on a darker beige stock (textured or with fibre content?) would be better—that combination to be sample-tested and reviewed, to ensure text legibility, for both front and back.

Initially expecting this book to be smaller than it turned out to be, I considered abandoning perfect bound (most common) in favour of having the book spine stapled. The book fattened up some and, inquiring, I found that the difference in binding cost was modest. Anyway, beyond that factor, I opted to stick with the perfect binding.

I expect to staple-bind a future book, one destined to contain fewer pages. A non-fiction book that has spent considerable time on a back burner is a local tale involves twelve years my wife spent on a Malahat farm, one located on lower Vancouver Island. After distributing copies to family and friends and perhaps selling a few, I may explore publisher interest in producing a revised, expanded, version of the book. Who knows...

Much of what appears above only reflects one perspective. Seek other experiences. Talk to several cover designers. Compare notes with other writers. Check the internet for data on the topic. The cover for each book tackled should be considered afresh. What was done previously should have little bearing on what's coming up, aside from winning factors. Be objective. What best suits the book's interior should decide the issue.

Cover sorted and completed, for those interested, it's now time to give some thought to all what's involved in self-publishing a book.

Self-Publishing

Unless your creation is non-fiction, of historical or local interest, original or unusual fiction, latching onto an agent or finding a publisher to accept even a well written and well presented manuscript is doubtful. Is unlikely. But do give it a go if making the attempt is important to you, is something you must do before you are prepared to turn to self-publishing for getting your creation into print.

Some writers have managed to achieve a rewarding publishing connection by attending writing conferences that offer sessions with agents, editors or publishers. Others try to contact potential recipients for the fruit of their efforts by email or even snail mail, the latter means now all but an obsolete method, one hardly worth the effort. Whatever the attempt, don't become upset because of a lack of response; that's far from unusual. After a while, being ignored or rejected becomes less stressful, easier to accept. Serious writers know both well.

Unknown writers, and those not represented by an agent (try to get one!), have little-to-no chance of accessing a traditional publisher. Unsolicited manuscripts seldom arrive on the desk of someone able to decide that a submission is worth a second glance. The majority are added to the slush pile, may be returned if a return envelope and postage was included in the package received. Or manuscripts may just vanish. Queries are treated little better.

To improve your chances of being accepted, or at least being considered, given more than a quick peek on the way by, research targeted firms to ensure that they deal with what you plan or wish to send along. A few potentials lined up, send the query to named individuals in those firms.

Smaller publishers tend to specialise: fiction or non-fiction, young children, teens, local or general history, environment, literary fiction, outdoor, adventure, other genres. Larger publishers may do the same or they may focus on mass-market general fiction; in hardcover, perfect bound or pocketbook formats.

Listings of publishers and some idea of what they deal in can be found at libraries or via the internet. Also check out *The Canadian Writer's Guide*.

Publishing organisations are nowadays even less receptive than a decade or so ago. Their circumstances have altered. Grants have dwindled and profitability has become more elusive. While some larger publishers do well, for others staying afloat is difficult. Many firms now publish no more than a handful of books per year and they focus on books that appear likely to succeed, produce a profitable sales volume.

If or when efforts to land a publisher prove unsuccessful, self-publishing your creation is an alternative that will get the job done, provided you are prepared to undertake what, even after the book is in print, amounts to a full-time job: market and distribute the book, take care of all those chores otherwise assumed and handled by a traditional publisher. On the plus side, in exchange for a considerable personal investment of time and effort, you gain total control of what you publish. You get to call the shots.

A fair trade-off? Perhaps. It all depends on how enthusiastic you are, or can become, about accepting self-publishing as the way to go. How prepared you are to tackle all that must be done. How competently you perform all the necessary chores. And, how well that initial enthusiasm holds up.

To repeat, the days of sending off a manuscript and waiting patiently for a response, or a package return that may never materialise, are no more. Nowadays email queries and writing samples are the preferred means, if that's at all considered worthwhile. And, with some publishers, email attachments may not be welcomed—check for submission guidelines. Query sent, be patient; don't expect too much, too soon.

Like manuscript submissions, email queries are often ignored. Frustrating, but then sending an email query isn't all that costly beyond the time and effort. Alternatives? Make the attempt, after carefully preparing what you intend to send. You might get lucky!

I recall sending a manuscript to an Ottawa agent decades ago, at a cost just short of twenty dollars. I never heard anything or ever saw the package again, despite pursuing the matter by letter. And, back then submissions had a better chance of getting some kind of response. My recollection correct, that typed submission may have been the only copy.

For those attempting to find publishers via the internet, check to see if there is a listing for your province, or others adjacent, or go nationwide. The scope is your decision, but you might get a better reception closer to home. For example, I found the Association of Book Publishers of British Columbia (members and associates): www.books.bc.ca.

No email address? How about sending a fax? Often a fax number is easier to find than an email address. Some versions of Windows (like XP) provide an optional fax facility that works with MS Word. No fax hardware aboard? Messages can also be faxed via the internet, at a cost.

Whatever the submission mode, ensure that what you send complies with submission guidelines found for the target firm. If possible, browse publication examples before crafting a query; and send it to a named individual (publisher or editor).

Being careless, overly wordy, aggressive or presumptuous could lose the game before it gets underway. Be polite. Curtail any excessively persistent inclinations. Improper follow-up action will waste any decent effort invested earlier.

For most publishers email contact is preferable to using the telephone. Responses, if any, should be respected: *no* means *no*! On the other hand, a convincing and creative, provocative and fresh, project-focused, positive yet respectful, approach might just work. A writer's everlasting mantra: I might get lucky!

Self-publishing your book, you'll be in good company. Others who've spent personal funds getting early creations into print include Beatrix Potter, John Grisham, James Joyce, Zane Grey, Steven King, Margaret Atwood and Ernest Hemmingway.

Unfortunately, self-published material still faces an uphill acceptance battle; with fiction in particular, although that appears to be easing up to some extent. Ensure that your creation is comparable to other similar books published. Invest the necessary time, browse books shelves in search of what you should end up with, what's needed to compete.

Despite the advantage of having total control and experiencing a shorter book generation time, self-publishing isn't for everyone. It requires a significant investment of time and effort, perhaps more participation than you want to contribute.

You'll have to orchestrate and manipulate myriad details on your own, unless family or friends can be coaxed into pitching in and sharing the load. Help in short supply or absent, you may have to pay others to deal with requirements beyond time availability, beyond your capacity or capability. If, however, you're bound to press onward, hopefully what follows will prove helpful.

A variety of self-publishing methods exist, may be available and acceptable. Vanity Press (you pay it all) has mutated over the years into forms of co-publishing (costs shared). Some firms get paid a fee upfront, charge for editing and such, provide some website marketing and offer books to an author at a price. Some even pay royalties. The ultimate accumulated cost can still be substantial.

POD (print on demand) publishers may suit some hopefuls. An upfront feed paid, further costs will depend upon what they do for you, what you ask them to do: editing, setup, cover, PDF file(s), expanded marketing schemes. Several people I know have followed this route and, cost aside, have been pleased with the results. They managed to get their creation into print, something unachievable on their own. As for website book marketing, are selling prices set according to the unit cost to an author for a book? If so, does a cost of $10 create a selling price at $25, and will buyers pay that for a novel by an unknown author?

With do-it-all-yourself self-publishing or where you do most of what must be done, with a little help where absolutely needed, the overall savings can be substantial. But, invested effort demands may counter those savings, in particular if the end product is found wanting.

External financial assistance may be available to help defray costs, but not to the extent once provided. Fiction grants in particular are hard to find nowadays but your project may qualify for one: federal, provincial, municipal or a contribution from an organisation or corporation. It's worth exploring—if you don't ask, you don't get!

E-books and the internet: Take care! What do you truly want or expect: a wider distribution of your work or to get paid for each and every book? In general the internet is a rather loosely governed distribution channel. Some websites may adequately control downloads; others may not. Ensure that any chosen distribution website meets your requirements and standards, that it includes some measure of protection against pilfering. For example, encrypted PDF book-files, so that book-text cannot be extracted as plain text for use otherwise or elsewhere.

Printing aside, there are a variety of ways to self-publish your material:

- Cover perhaps excluded, do it all yourself on a computer, aided by what your wordprocessor can accomplish.
- Deliver no more than a manuscript to a POD (print on demand) publisher or a book organiser, along with cover-content ideas and perhaps a picture or sketch.
- Actually produce the book-interior PDF (Adobe's portable document format) file and have someone else create the cover and provide its PDF.
- Also do the cover if feasible and with access to appropriate software.
- Or, perhaps a blending of what you are able to do with what others can do better, at a cost you can afford.

Self-publishing firms and some added-capability printers are prepared to pitch in. Talk to a few and find out what they can provide, at what cost, and what they'd require from you.

Before seeking a POD publisher or perhaps an added-facility printer, gather as much information as possible. Consider upcoming decisions regarding your creation, important choices that will have to be made at some point—by someone, likely you: book size, target number of pages, paper weight, hardcover or soft, binding method, fonts and sizes, cover design concept and layout (laminated or not). Knowing what lies ahead, what must be anticipated, may well initiate a change of heart or intentions.

What you intend to do with the end product may determine what's best in the circumstances. Books or booklets intended for distribution to family and friends require a more modest structural setup and less content organising and polishing. A wordprocessor alone may be all that's needed to complete the whole project.

For a creation that you expect people to buy, spend money on, a decided upgrade in structure and content, more spit and polish, are needed; as are added tools or talents, some of which may be beyond what you can provide.

The selling price; got one in mind? If not, visit bookshops and scan the shelves for books similar to what you intend or have all but completed. Bear in mind your writing status, where you potentially rank (or don't) amidst other writers. Then settle on a price, one that may not be what you'd like to get, but one that's realistic in the circumstances, one that'll sell some books. Hardcover most unlikely, few fiction offerings by an unknown author merit a price in excess of $20. Unless unique and fresh, nor do many non-fiction books for those just starting out. Price for this book?

Done your best, gone as far as you can get? Decided that you've had enough and require help that you are now willing to pay for; assistance that you can afford? Already tried a savvy friend you persuaded to scrutinise content, but disappointed with the results? Need an editor after all, but don't know one, or someone who can recommend one?

Self-published books, with regard to editing, differ little from books produced by firms devoted to book publication. They too can benefit from a fresh perspective, perhaps to a greater extent. It's hard to do the writing and then try to be a hard-nosed editor, be brutal if you can manage to adopt that alter-attitude and have the capability.

Now inclined toward obtaining an independent scrutiny of your material? Decide how much you are able or prepared to spend and which editing options you feel are needed, what you expect for your dollars: a proofread for grammar and spelling, structural comment, content assessment, a full-scale edit. Make a list of expectations and other particular items for later discussion with a potential editor.

In search of assistance candidates, check info provided by the Editors' Association of Canada (branches across Canada): www.editors.ca. Identify those persons appearing a better fit for your project. Contact one, two or three and discuss the project, ensuring that you are well aware of each and every potential cost involved.

Settle on an editor and be prepared to enter into an agreement. A standard form is available. Understand the standard inclusions and ponder each and every exception proposed. Ask dumb questions—are there any? Is there a good reason for each deviation, one acceptable to you? Do you have an agreement change or two in mind? Compromise may be required. If in doubt, run the proposed contract by a lawyer experienced in the field (added cost?).

Self-publishing a book, beyond achieving decent results in the circumstances, requires a business sense, a willingness and capability to deal with all the nitty-gritty: book wrapping, shipping or delivery, price discounting and billing, distribution tracking and query, payment follow up, bookkeeping. How well you do it all will determine the measure of your success: few books sold or an additional printings needed to satisfy demand, or somewhere between the two. The initial goal is to receive more cash than expended.

It's not for me to rate the quality of my writing efforts, but I do have an edge in tackling other aspects of self-publishing. My accounting and business background have proven handy, as has having a practical perspective. But is a marriage of the two, writing and taking care of business, a workable combination for most writers? Could you tackle both?

To make life easier and move the project forward, determine what you are aware of and what you are not. Ask lots of questions, of lots of people. Again, there's no such thing as a dumb question. And, what you learn from one person may come in handy when dealing with another.

Or, you might encounter an advantageous situation or circumstance waiting to be exploited. For instance, while pursuing an unrelated matter, I learned about the funds available through registering for Public Lending Rights, dollars paid annually for books found in libraries.

I also discovered websites where I could register books so that title and author info are available to potential readers or other book purchasers (expanded detail, later this section).

Upfront, estimate the number of books that you think you can dispose of. Use that as a base for determining how many books to order: a few to start off, a defendable larger number produced by batch production (lower unit price?). Bear in mind that a great cost per unit isn't much of a benefit if too many copies end up piled in a corner, there to gather dust, because you didn't have a battle plan, some idea of how to get rid of them, or found the content wanting. A great price achieved by ordering more books loses it appeal if you later discover too many errors in that first batch and decide you have to reprint the book.

Income?

No matter how you manage to get your self-published book into print, selling copies won't fill your pockets with cash unless you change your name to that of a well-known, successful, writer and are able to write like the one you chose.

Many but not necessarily all distributors will expect a hefty discount. As will bookshops, which will also likely expect a book or books to be left on consignment (tattered returns?).

And, if you fail to bill shipping costs, what remains can drop to less than half the book's cover price. How would that compare to your cost? Read received purchase orders carefully and bill mailing costs unless arranged otherwise to your satisfaction.

Few scribes make a living writing. Most would starve if not for day-job earnings.

Back in the 1980s the average annual income from writing was said to be five thousand dollars, with a sizeable number of writing efforts producing nothing, with many writers out of pocket for their efforts.

Nowadays writers are likely worse off. Writing ranks have swollen as available market outlets dwindled. Does selling five thousand trade book copies in a year qualify as a Canadian bestseller? Is the average annual book sale in the much larger U.S. market only two thousand copies?

For most wannabe writers and those who've managed to achieve some measure of success but aren't attempting to make a living at it, getting a book into print could be considered an expensive yet gratifying ego trip, one often fraught with disappointment.

Assuming that having a publisher's name on the cover and title page of a self-published book has value (book acceptability, perhaps a taxation advantage), you may wish to create your own publishing label. Where you are, locate the source or where you have to go to get what's needed. Here in Victoria, details and the forms needed to organise a proprietorship can be obtained from the Ministry of Finance, situated by the downtown central library branch.

To get a better idea of financial implications for writing, obtain a small business booklet (GST details included) from the nearest Canada Revenue Agency or by a mailed request. In Victoria the CRA building is located on Vancouver Street.

If you intend to set yourself up as a publisher (sole proprietor) and anticipate reporting results on your annual income tax return, contact an accountant and discuss expectations with her or him.

A publishing label established, for the book refer to yourself (as author) in the third person (John Smith or he... rather than I...).

Heading into the creation and distribution of your book (or books) it's best to know how things are going. Be aware of financial progress or lack thereof. No matter how guesstimated, prepare an initial operating budget and amend it as necessary during the venture. Be sure to include after-book-printing costs such as shipping, workspace and supplies, travel and promotion.

Use a columnar pad or a spreadsheet program like Excel and compare actual results with expectations. Few initial considerations or decisions will remain unchanged but having some idea about where you are headed, and how you hope to get there, may help sort out unexpected matters that are bound to pop up along the way.

Expecting to make money from an early undertaking is unrealistic. And, that may also apply to subsequent creations. Who can predict the future and what success it may deliver. The only reward you may receive is the satisfaction of seeing the results of your efforts in print.

In any case, you'll need to keep track of income and expenses, or pay someone to do so. If you plan to handle the chore, a columnar pad or a spreadsheet program works well for this purpose. For added detail, check out the section on monitoring activity.

Printing

The book-printing world has changed in the last decade or so, more dramatically than it did through many years before. POD (digital print on demand production) has made self-publishing easier. For some folk the price is acceptable; for other it's beyond what's affordable. Alternate approaches? Invest the time, explore printing options. POD? Batch printing? To get a handle on what's available, try to get competitive quotes for an estimated quantity and anticipated book structure. More books: a lesser unit cost but a larger overall dollar layout. More pages: a higher cost. My three novels and this book were all batch-printed, one by a publisher in Toronto, three by me, here in Victoria.

Unless a more-distant firm is offering a deal that's irresistible, one considered valid and workable, seek a local firm for added convenience (access, delivery, pickup) and perhaps, all considered, a reduced cost. To compare, a few U.S. options: www.pendiumpublishing.com > www.xulonpress.com > www.iuniverse.com > www.infinitypublishing.com. However, contacting such sources may establish a link that'll pester you in future.

While the long established batch-print quantity-ordering practice persists, POD publishers/printers have gained, are yet gaining, popularity. They offer the advantage of no ordering quantity issue to struggle with. But is the overall cost acceptable? If so, forge ahead, order a modest number of copies and see how they sell or move out on consignment.

If you later find that you've been more successful than anticipated, print more copies. Another batch if that's the original means chosen. Doing so will be a pleasure, even if there's a unit cost increase.

Ordering smaller quantities at the outset at added cost also permits correcting any serious errors discovered and then printing additional copies lacking those mistakes. How many errors are acceptable?

Assuming that fixed expenses such as the outlay for cover creation are absorbed by an initial batch-print run (the original expectation), the per-copy cost on reorder could be considered reduced, thus permitting copies to be sold based upon a lesser cost. Would that expand distribution opportunities? Perhaps not a realistic calculation but it may alter perspective.

POD publishers like Trafford Publishing, with international operations, print a customer-ordered book locally (Canada, US, elsewhere), as and where ordered, thus saving shipping costs (a significant cost item). Such firms also offer website listings of books they produce. Whether or not that suits your requirements depends upon the breadth of book distribution you wish to achieve, expect to be able to exploit: local, countrywide, across this continent, around the world.

If you've found a POD publishing or batch-printing firm that appears ready and able to address your needs, be diligent. Find out what you'll get for how much money. Ask to see samples similar to what you have in mind. Consider checking the level of satisfaction for other customers of the firm. Query anything unclear or run such items by someone you know with related experience. Copyright. Restrictions. Marketing assistance. Other issues.

To repeat, and if applicable, is the cost-based-calculated selling price (eg 2.5 times cost) imposed by some POD publishers realistic? Will it provide a decent volume of book sales? For example, if a book cost works out to be $10 for the author, would someone pay $25 for the book?

Regarding book-production costs, when calculating the cost per book, do include everything you've spent. For a book worked on by a printer or POD publisher, that includes whatever's paid up front and during the process to anyone, plus the cost to the author for copies. Divide the total figure by the number of copies obtained (or expected to be obtained, if defendable).

For many scribes, arriving at the unit cost will be a shocker. For others who've handled some of the work preceding the actual printing, that unit cost may be less disturbing.

How much is seeing your book in print worth to you?

Too many writers make little or no money. Some achieve no more than a reduction of losses. Whatever they take off the cover price deepens their losses, as does handing out free copies to family and friends, a reviewer or to others as found necessary.

For more detail regarding income or lack thereof, refer to the section on flogging that creation.

Exposure

There's no free ride, not now, not ever. To sell books, there's always work to be done. Make a list, with emphasis given to how you plan to gain the attention of the buying public. Don't underrate that necessity. Consider options, thinking outside the box as some say. Talk to other writers and explore the topic via the internet.

For a self-published book, is any free exposure, good or not-so-good publicity, worth pursuing? Will it produce helpful contacts? Whatever the determination, accept that any results will be beyond your control.

To dispose of copies buyers have to be aware of, be exposed to, the existence of your book. Get copies into some bookshops, despite discounting and consignment issues. While selling to libraries may deter book sales to individuals, doing so does provide exposure, and may produce a few Public Lending Rights dollars.

Join an association organised around your genre. Someone I know did so and obtained outstanding publication assistance. Whatever the degree of involvement, do ask lots of questions in search of unusual promotional possibilities.

Check to see if a daily paper or another popular local publication provides a daily, weekly or monthly section catering to books. If so, does it include a brief outline of self-published books? My third novel was mentioned in such a column. A decade or two ago such acknowledgement of self-published material, in particular fiction, would not have occurred unless the content was spectacular, had already gained some measure of public attention.

If many of the books printed on the first run remain on hand beyond a reasonable span of time, be prepared to discount that cover price. Few self-publishers early on manage to flog their books at cover price. Family and friends may expect a concession (or a freebie). You'll have to tempt browsers at craft fairs. Bookshops and distributors expect that forty-percent discount (or perhaps more).

As for sending copies out in hopes of having an established reviewer appraise what you have created and provide a glowing or lesser review, don't waste the books. Without a handy contact to bolster your efforts, your chances are slim to none. Media folk are flooded with requests and an awaited response may never arrive. Those folk tend to review what they expect will appeal to a majority of their readers. Non-fiction, in particular how-to guides, may have a better chance. In any case, any query to a newspaper or magazine editor or reporter/writer should be brief but comprehensive (catchy opener, appealing synopsis, author info). Who knows, you might get lucky.

Other Stuff

Whether or not you are prepared to do most or all of what's initially needed, there are matters that must be attended to—by someone. Promote and sell. Visit shops. Contact libraries. Attend book fairs. Wrap and label. Ship or deliver. Bill and collect. Keep track of book traffic and money.

And there are a few other matters to consider (first two items to be addressed before printing):

➢ Obtain from Collections Canada an ISBN number – www.collectionscanada.ca/isbn/index-e.html – can be arranged via the internet by email.

➢ Then file for a Collection Canada CIP registration – www.collectionscanda.ca/cip/index-e.html – requires an ISBN number (now thirteen digits) and additional information (copy of title page, publication date, price, content summary—back cover info?). Processing details and an application form and instructions can be downloaded from the website. Depending upon the number of books initially printed, one or two book copies are to be sent to Legal Deposit, National Library of Canada in Ottawa, along with a completed form (can be obtained from the website or otherwise requested).

- ➢ If your books will be found in libraries you can register with the Public Lending Rights Commission and perhaps receive royalties (based on a summer library audit). PLR registration: www.plr-dpp.ca. Open for application each year, between mid February and the first of May. Once registered, you should receive a title update sheet in following years. Best to publish in December or January for a later copyright date?
- ➢ Canadian Books in Print. This used to be Canada-based but now has been integrated into Bowkerlink in U.S: bip.bowkerlink@bowker.com. For info: www.bowker.com, www.bowkerlink.com.
- ➢ BC Bookworld – www.abcbookworld.com – a west coast author database.

Assuming you're on your own and doing all that's needed, after completing the large file, scrutinise it to ensure that all structural errors are found and fixed. Anything missed will carry forward into the PDF file (see next section). Errors discovered post-conversion may have to be corrected in the original file and that would require another PDF conversion, at added cost if you are paying someone else for that service.

When I set out to arrange all that was needed to convert my manuscript for a second novel into a book, I scanned writing-related publications and then turned to the yellow pages. What I discovered was confusing but helpful. What was offered ran the gambit, from printing and nothing more to cover assistance and on up to organising, producing, the whole project. Ultimately I narrowed the field and settled upon two printing options. The firm I settled upon also provided cover creation.

And now, on to what's needed to get that PDF file that printers want...

PDF Preparation

What is a PDF and as a writer why should I care?

While not the assortment encountered in earlier years, writers and others nowadays still use differing computers: PCs with Windows, MACs with their operating system, computers running on UNIX. The prime benefit of a PDF file conversion is the creation of a common file format, one that remains the same no matter the computer platform. And, to print your book, it's what a printing firm wants.

Adobe Acrobat creates a PDF (portable document format) file by converting what was created or compiled within a wordprocessor or similar program. After conversion, unless renamed, the file retains the same root name, ending with '.pdf.'. Such a conversion isn't accomplished with Adobe Reader, a free utility that'll display or print PDF files (download from www.adobe.com).

If interested in PDF-conversion software, don't run out and buy Adobe Acrobat. First, check with computer-savvy friends to see if they have the means and can do the conversion for you. Or seek a solution via the internet, pursue product reviews or software user comments for other converters, to determine that they will do what's needed, at a lesser or no cost. Check out CutePDF Writer (free download) or seek info on Scansoft or Nuance. Or, check out the wordprocessor in Open Office (free download).

Adobe Acrobat, beyond creating PDF files of value to writers, has other talents and uses. Its files are found on websites for displaying text and can be structured as interactive files that'll accept data input. If curious, check the website for product details or visit a library and browse the computer section shelves in search of a how-to guide for the product.

I have an older version of Adobe Acrobat but have yet to read most sections of the self-help guide I acquired. My interest in the program is restricted to its conversion capabilities, as used for books. That capability is what's outlined in this section. For some writers—in particular those who will have someone else do the conversion—some details may be more than they want or need to know.

What follows assumes that book sections or chapters are individual files, created that way for ease of organization and handling. If that's not the case, section breaks and whatever will have to be managed within the larger file.

A passing note! If this isn't your first book don't just forge ahead, basing the new one on any that preceded it; seek improved presentation. Does this book differ from the previous one? If so, should that change be reflected or incorporated into the structure of this one? Even if the book is unchanged in content or concept there may have been something you missed with a previous one.

Bear in mind that whichever portions of the book-creation task you handle on your own will save you dollars. Do try to perform some of what's required, necessary, to achieving that print-ready file stage and get within sight of that anticipated book in hand.

Ahead of attempting the manuscript-files combining process, if you don't have one, purchase one (or more, content differs) of those handy and informative how-to helpmates for your wordprocessor. Keep it handy after having read and re-read appropriate portions. That'll help sort out what must be done and when. Program-use assistance is also available via an upper-screen icon or the keyboard's [F1] key.

Unless the book size is to be left at 8.5 by 11 inches, the number of pages will expand as manuscript files are converted into smaller book-size pages. The ultimate number will be influenced by: margin widths, header and footer accommodation, opening chapter identification positioning and spacing. In short, anything that expands blank page space will jack up the ultimate number of pages, perhaps to a doubling or more.

For my second novel, including pages unnumbered, the increase reached 84% and, as altered for the third one, almost a doubling. For this book, as organised, the expansion exceeded a doubling. All three books were 5.5 by 8.5 inches in size.

Decide upon a page size, one commonly used best. A size of 5.5 by 8.5 inches is popular (my apologies for using inches but I'm an old guy, one inch = 2.5 centimetres). With smaller pages, how will portions of the content fit within the revised format?

Are there any pictures, sketches or list headings that will necessitate shifting text to achieve proper page positioning? Or perhaps there's a block of text that should appear intact on one page. Watch for such items when completing a book-size pass through the material.

A layout example: In my last novel I used line 4 for chapter numbers (40-point Comic Sans) and started chapter text on line 12 (10-point Bookman Old Style). Dedication, previous books and contact info on the back of the first page inside (on front: story synopsis?) were centered (10-point Bookman OS). I used the same sans serif font on the title page, but larger and in bold. The back of the title page contained centred publication-related information: copyright, disclaimer, ISBN number and CIP detail, where printed.

The text font size used on the first page (book info) and the back cover was larger (Bookman OS, 12-point) than what was used in chapters. While I admit to missing this one, any back-of-the-book author page or description should perhaps adopt a font smaller than what was adopted for chapter text. While a 12-point font may be similar used in this book, the section text is 11-point rather than 10-point for easier reading, in particular for those in my age bracket.

Combining Chapters

Before tackling the actual combining of the manu-script section files, you may wish to do a test run to sort out what must be done and how. For instance, once introduced, do headers or footers need to be added section by section, chapter by chapter? During a test run make notes of discoveries to clarify and assist the actual combining of chapter files. For the title page and other pages before and after those numbered (chapter text), setup requirements will differ.

With the synopsis, intro page or title page (first page in book) onscreen and altered to the smaller size, scan and adjust content for fit and layout, then SAVE AS it. Name the new file 'book07' (or whatever suits). Insert a section break (INSERT > BREAK: section, next page) at the end of that file and add the next section plus another section break. When a prologue or first chapter is the next portion to add, pre-adjust it for page setup (margins, paper size, layout, justification and hyphenation. Then add headers and/or footers (first time only?).

All in order, insert the next chapter and add a section break, then adjust and insert the next one, and so on until the book is fully assembled. Unnumbered sections or pages at the end of the book will require the same treatment applied to the opening unnumbered book pages. The process is further detailed later in this section.

If errors or problems arise during the test run, go back to the drawing board (as some say) and start over, keeping an eye on those notes you made, or should have made. A successful test run completed, you're ready to proceed with the real thing, the actual compilation procedure.

Does all that appear a tad complicated? It'll seem that way until clarified by actually doing it, going through the steps involved: slowly, one by one. That's the reason for suggesting a trial run, perhaps using shrunken files (delete middle portions) created by first copying originals (SAVE AS) to a new name (test, test2). Trial and error will bring to light the proper approach—that assisted by frequent dips into that wordprocessor how-to guide that by now should be starting to show mild signs of wear and tear.

As do many others, I use Microsoft Word for creating documents, including book files. Not a task-oriented desktop publishing program, MS Word may or may not do everything on your wish list. At times it may not function as expected—keep an eye out for problems or errors that may pop up during the combining progress.

For example, using Word 2000 and Windows XP for my third novel, the combining steps produced errors, unwanted changes: fonts altered in type and size, bold text appeared... For a previous book I used Word97 with Windows 98 and encountered no such aggravation, did not have to spend time correcting errors not created by me.

Whatever errors or problems appear, they should be corrected before adding another section, must be corrected before PDF conversion. Go through the finished package once, twice and then again, as many times as it takes to be satisfied that all's as it should be.

A book-size run through in print layout view (VIEW > PRINT LAYOUT) could offer a different perspective (shows headers and footers) and provide an opportunity to check page content and positioning. That's what I did for my last book-size, pre-conversion, run through this book's content.

Unless you have the necessary software or money to burn, remember that correcting errors discovered post-PDF-conversion could necessitate another conversion. To clarify what can be corrected within the PDF file or not, ask your chosen printer.

Avoid disappointment, unrecoverable and wasted cost. Invest your time where and when it counts—before PDF conversion and later book printing.

As previously mentioned, the combining process is defined according to how MS Word functions. If you use other software or don't have a self-help book for your wordprocessor, get one and clarify detail that differs from what appears here. Also, you may wish to expand upon anything encountered that requires clarification. Covering minute detail—what can be better provided by onscreen help accessed by the [F1] key or within a self-help guide—was never intended.

Important!!! Before mucking about with your precious files, ensure that they are fully backed up, to a couple floppy disks, one or more DVDs or CDs, or a USB/flash/jump drive—and yes, I do mean multiple backups. Book files aren't easy to replace. Computers and storage devices can and do fail. Keeping copies elsewhere, remote from where the computer sits if feasible, is a good idea, in case of fire. I know folk who had no backups and lost a whole book because of an unexpected computer mishap. Don't let that happen to you! Computer gear, like people, can let you down.

If I sound a bit paranoid about backup, it's because I probably am. I even back up a file I'm currently working on (to one disk) if I've been working on an important file for a while or a lengthy session is interrupted. Who knows when something might go amiss? Saving the file and copying to a disk sure beats having to try to remember and re-enter what likely cannot all be recalled. Why lose any of it.

If using clipart or sketches that differ in size for chapter openings (with or without numbers or other section identifying detail), print the first page of each chapter and compare for layout: set one page aside another to ensure that, for the sake of appearance, the pages appear compatible and that the first row of text starts on the same line or close to it.

Well...the manuscript is shipshape, is as good as it's going to get. It's now time to rearrange the material and convert it into the chosen book size. Actually in my case, the first text section of this book was already that way; that's how I tested alternatives for, and settled page layout (margins...). To leave the files in manuscript form (or almost) where they resided, I copied edited sections and combined them in another folder, one I'd labelled 'book-combo' for that purpose.

Before proceeding to the actual PDF conversion, make sure that all non-numbered sections are complete and up to date. If the 'author page' should be positioned as an odd, right-hand, page, is it? Are ISBN/CIP details or other items on the back of the title page as they should be? If there's a contents listing, does it include correct book-sized page numbers?

Within Windows Explorer:
- Located in the folder where the book files reside, copy files to 'book-combo.' EDIT > SELECT ALL –or– [Ctrl]+[A] on the keyboard to highlighted all files. To get the files to 'book-

combo,' right click on the block of files, drag to 'book-combo' and choose 'copy.'

- Move to the 'book-combo' folder and delete unwanted files, those not intended to be part of the book's interior (cover, layout, test files, etc). Click on the first unwanted file and then, holding down the [Ctrl] key, click each of the others. All unwanted items highlighted, tap the [Delete] key and respond 'Yes' to prompt.
- Remaining files the correct ones, combine sections as outlined below.

The Conversion Process in More Detail

Before tackling the actual combination process, ensure that the layout for all chapters/sections and other pages are as they should be. That done, for the first file, within Page Setup (FILE > PAGE SETUP):

- Tick the Mirror Margins box.
- Set margins. Example, this book (inches): top/1.3, bottom/.9, inside/.9, outside/.6. gutter/0 (inside margin expanded instead), header/.8, footer/.5.
- Via the Paper Size tab, set paper size (5.5 by 8.5 inches popular).
- Via the Layout tab, tick 'differing odd/even' and 'different first page' boxes.
- Select/highlight all text and block justify it: click squared lines item to right in upper bar.
- Accessed via TOOLS > LAUGUAGE > HYPHENATION, tick the 'automatically hyphenate' box and accept the default setting or alter the setting to suit.

- Via VIEW > HEADER and FOOTER, for at least the first section requiring them, enter header(s) and/or footer(s): left, right or centred; top and/or bottom, smaller or differing font? Both a header and footer (smaller font, sans serif, non-bold) were used for this book. A previous book only had headers—for odd-numbered pages, a page number and author name; for even-numbered pages book title and page number. Dashes and spaces separated numbers from text.
- To review results: FILE > PRINT PREVIEW or VIEW > PRINT LAYOUT.
- During the combining process, as each task is completed and found to be as expected, SAVE the file: (FILE > SAVE or [Ctrl]+[S] – hold down first key and tap the second.
- Repeat the above for each chapter, header/footer setup perhaps not repeated.

All found satisfactory, it's time to move on to the combining task. Page or section break? For the most part using a section break will be the choice, but for the early pages and those at the end of the book, a page break may suit (experiment during a test run?).

Ready to go:
- Make a list of files to combine, and tick those off as the combining progresses. Take care not to duplicate any file added, not miss any.
- Pages front and back should be unnumbered. Those numbered: chapters and any introduction or prologue or epilogue, excepting the first page of each chapter.

- SAVE AS the first section, under another name (book07?).
- Add a section break (INSERT > BREAK): section, next page.
- Add another section (INSERT > FILE): early book pages, then numbered sections, followed by back pages. Ensure that each portion added appears as intended, before saving the big file and moving on to the next addition.
- Add a section break (INSERT > BREAK): section, next page.
- While combining files, SAVE the file manually once an added section is judged to be as it should be.
- Repeat the process until all sections and odd pages of the manuscript are combined and in the proper order.

While scanning the resulting smaller-sized-page file for discrepancies, watch for items (pictures, clipart, headings, blocks of text) that should appear intact on one page. To achieve proper positioning, text may have to be shifted between pages. While it would be ideal to have each display alongside text that deals with it, that isn't always possible. If necessary, items displayed can be identified and referred to within describing text (exhibit 12: brief description or caption).

To check for anticipated positioning results in the big file: FILE > PRINT PREVIEW or VIEW > PRINT LAYOUT. Normally working in VIEW > NORMAL (shows page and section breaks), to display header(s) or footer(s) (page numbering, odd/even differences) try FILE > PRINT PREVIEW or VIEW > PRINT LAYOUT.

Repeated because it's important: throughout the routine, back up those precious files, to multiple media if possible.

To repeat: Throughout the exercise, check results and then check them again, as each and every step is taken and completed. Things can go wrong, will go wrong and mishaps may not be attributable to keyboard activity. Scrutinize each section added and fix any glitches before saving the big file at that point and proceeding with the next addition. And, do try to assess what appears on pages with a fresh eye, one remote from the gal or guy who wrote the material.

If your manuscript is already one big file, with page numbering never used or already removed, it will have to be processed and adjusted if need be to end up with what's ultimately required prior to a PDF-conversion. Adjusted to book size, the file will have to be formatted and sectioned where needed as outlined above (INSERT > BREAK...), with attention paid to ensure that unnumbered and numbered pages end up as intended, as commonly found in most books.

All files combined? Great! Now, go through the big file again, in search of errors or items missed earlier, things that didn't end up as anticipated. Are:
- front pages as they should be?
- any chapters duplicated, added twice by mistake?
- all fonts and sizes as intended?
- headers or footers where and as expected?

- all chapter opening text lines where they should be on the page?
- indents consistent, as and where expected?
- all paragraphs properly justified?
- margins properly shifting from left to right according to odd/even pages?
- pictures or sketches situated properly on all pages?
- any glaring blank page gaps fixed?
- back pages as intended, author page odd numbered (if wanted that way)?

Error possibilities are manifold: check the whole package, line by line, page by page, section by section. Last chance! If someone else has contributed to the material, by way of review or edit, check that also. After the book's printed, who is responsible for what matters little.

Am I overstating concern? Perhaps, but not the situation, the importance of making sure all is correct. For the two books I self-edited, I screened pages several times and still missed items. Remember that, after the PDF conversion and the book is printed, any and all mistakes found will diminish the value of all that time and effort you invested.

Something similar created for a previous book, what follows is a guidance page used for this book. Intended to assist in keeping track of what needed doing, when and how, I revised page content for what I discovered during the project.

WRITING: WHAT'S GOOD, BAD AND UGLY - NOTES, BEFORE COMBINING SECTIONS (differing formats, pages numbered or not) but after ensuring that for the top of each first section page the first text line is on the same or within one line of others, that spacing for the clipart sits right and is the same for spacing as others that are identical: scattered words, maze, books. Print and compare first pages for sections.

FOR SECTIONS:

(1) JUSTIFY: select all text and click on squared icon on tool bar, top right + then check for (+ fix) items within the section that should not adopt that justification setting.

(2) TOOLS > LANGUAGE > HYPHENATION: tick 'automatically hyphenate document' and accept hyphenation default of .4 [choose another?]

(3) FILE > PAGE SETUP
Margins tab: tick Mirror margins and set: top/1.3, btm/.9, in/.9, out/.6, gtr/0, h/.8, f/.5

Paper size tab: 5.5 x 8.5, inches

Layout tab: ticks for different odd/even, different first page

>SECTION OKAY, SAVE HERE<

FOR FIRST NUMBERED SECTION:

(3) VIEW > HEADER and FOOTER: centre header and footer, non-bold CSans/9pt, leave first page blank, set even header to 'D.G. Wilkes,' set odd header to 'Writing: What's Good, Bad and Ugly,' set both footers to # (select from h/f bar options)

>SECTION OKAY, SAVE HERE<

(4) All okay, INSERT > PAGE BREAK, ticking next page box

(5) INSERT > FILE, add next section

** AS COMBING SECTIONS – WATCH FOR AND FIX ERRORS SPOTTED **

TICK TWICE: COMBINING, SECTION OKAY

title page		contents		intro		1	2
3	4	5	6	7	8	9	
10	11	12					

last page/author -> force odd page setting, if needed.

(6) All combined, complete 'contents' page for section-start page numbers

Before tackling the PDF Conversion, are you satisfied that all is okay? Any blocks of inserted text that didn't end up as expected? If included, has any contents listing page numbers been dealt with (after no more page shifting or corrections made or to be made)? Has ISBN/CIP data received been added to the back of the title page, exactly as received? To ease the insertion of that data, if received by email, select, copy and paste (or keyboard equivalents) what's needed from the email response.

Creating the PDF File

Converting the big file doesn't alter it. A new file with a '.pdf' extension/ending, is created. PDF file in hand (no matter who creates it), scan the results (Adobe Reader) to see what, if anything, went awry. All found in order and ready to go, copy the content PDF file onto a DVD, CD or other media intended to go to the printer, along with any supporting material: hard-copy of ISBN number for barcode.

Add the cover PDF to the same media, or pass along media supplied by a cover designer, if available. If not, supply what's needed (sketch, written input) for the creation of a book cover.

When Adobe Acrobat software is installed, it attaches a tool bar to MS Word and becomes a file creating option within that program. For a conversion, you can choose to use the Adobe icon on the bar or the print option that appears in the popup-box list when you initiate a printing of the combined and sectioned manuscript file. The latter option works better for a book conversion.

Tackling the job not your cup of tea? Then ask around for a friend or someone allied to the writing business with the software needed to convert the file. Any fee for the conversion will be a fraction of what it'd cost to buy the program, an outlay unwarranted unless you anticipate frequent use, enjoy new challenges or are eager to accumulate software.

Adobe Acrobat uses Distiller (a popup-box print option) to create a PDF file. PDF files created with Distiller maintain formatting and fonts, graphics and photographic images of the original document no matter the computer or operating system encountered, assuming that the destination computer/printing system handles a PDF file.

Within MS Word, printing option selected for creating the PDF file:

- FILE > PRINT –or- [Ctrl]+[P] (hold down first key, tap second)
- Print-to Acrobat Distiller
- Click the Properties button to open the Distiller printer properties dialogue box
- Click the Adobe PDF Settings tab
- Conversion settings: choose 'print'
- Within Edit conversion settings: 'custom' and set page size as 5.5 x 8.5 inches or another size chosen
- Save as 'print(1)' or whatever number next appears
- Click OK
- In the Save PDF File dialogue box, accept the same name for the PDF or pick another

While the conversion routine went smoothly for a previous book using Word 97 and Windows 98), with Word 2000 and Windows XP trying to set the page size to 5.5" x 8.5" didn't work for my version of Adobe Acrobat.

What to do? Accessing Adobe's website, I found information about PDF files not retaining a custom page size.

Checking for related information within the Microsoft website (articles 282474, 157172), what I discovered, in part:

Issue - PDF files don't retain custom page sizes (Acrobat 5.x)

An Adobe PDF file has a standard page size (for example, Letter) instead of the custom page size of the document from which it was created. The PDF file was created in Windows XP, 2000 or NT 4.0. The original document was created in an application that doesn't write its own PostScript code (for example, Microsoft Word). If you created the PDF file from a Microsoft Word 2000 document using PDFMaker (Convert to AdobePDF) or Acrobat Distiller printer, Word returned the error "The margins of section 1 are set outside the printable area of the page. Do you want to continue?"

Solution 1

Create a new form in the Print Server Properties dialog box, and then re-create the PDF file:

1. Choose Start > Settings > Printers.
2. Select Acrobat Distiller.
3. Choose File > Server Properties.
4. Select Create a New Form.
5. Type a new name in the Form Description For text box.
6. Type the desired dimensions under Paper Size.
7. Click Save the Form.
8. Re-create the PDF file.

For Word 2000 and XP in my case, to fix the problem: CONTROL PANEL > PRINTERS > FILE > SERVER PROPERTIES. I set the name at 'book,' the page size as 5.5" x 8.5" and that did the trick. I was back in business.

To reiterate: Despite avid scrutiny, what may pop up in files during the combining and conversion process can boggle the mind. I missed a few items but all those problems were my fault. No matter, I had the conversion software at hand and having to re-convert the big file added a bit of effort but no cost. The message, for me...and for you: be diligent, it pays! You cannot go through that big file too many times.

Getting Printing Quotes

So, the PDF for the book's interior is finished. What next? Time to get some printing and binding prices. For my first self-published book I browsed the phone book's yellow pages and dug through my files for any adverts I'd extracted from related magazines. With some idea of what I wanted in mind (cover, interior), I chose five or six to pursue. For a variety of reasons I boiled those down to two, firms that best appeared to provide what I sought, what I thought I needed. Both firms were local and professed to produce books.

Contacting those two again I provided specs and requested prices. Prices obtained from the two were similar but only one of them would produce the cover PDF file—that contribution at a lesser cost than other providers I'd explored.

Content with the results for that book, for the next one I returned to the same firm, didn't get another price quote. Perhaps I could have saved a few dollars by getting a competitive quote but I opted to continue with a known entity, one I'd found satisfactory.

The price quote request (by email) content for this book:

- Title: Writing, What's Good, Bad and Ugly
- Size: 5.5 x 8.5 inch, perfect bound
- Cover stock: med.buff/brown, textured or fibre content (scan samples)
- Cover: print: darker brown (compare stock/print combo)

- Cover (back): barcode
- Cover: perhaps laminated (cover appearance without?)
- Paper: thinner, as for last book (Coming Up Short)
- Number of pages: *245* (more accurate number late advised)
- PDFs: I'll provide, interior and cover, on CD
- Quantity: ??? copies (actual number advised)
- Note(1): ISBN 978-0-9737633-2-4
- Note(2): extra cover, flat & I get proof copy at end

For the cover, at the firms place of business, I planned to consider potential stock samples and selected a suitable shade of buff/brown for the cover, gave thought to a cover/printing combination that produced a decent blending of the two for a cover that would appeal to buyers.

Or, would a coating of a buff colour add sufficient sheen to address what I was seeking? What do you think of the results? Decent. Not. How would you have done it differently?

Why the extra cover, flat? It could be scanned in and converted to a handy computer file. One for a previous book provided cover-shot attachments for emails (or embedded in a fax) sent to libraries and bookshops.

A card-backed cover copy ended up hanging in a back car window (with 'library?' added). Publicity is publicity, and every bit's needed to move books. The one in the car window was hung on a suction-cup hook so my wife could remove it when she drove the car. She failed to share my book-marketing zeal!

The proof copy had previously proven handy for recording any errors or items for future alteration considerations.

For the previous two books (novels) I provided an idea of what I wanted, together with supporting sketches for the cover. For this book I supplied the PDF for the cover.

Proof copy ready, I perused the ensemble for earlier books on the printer's premises. For this book, due to its nature (non-fiction, topic, a higher standard?), I planned to take it home for a more relaxed scrutiny of interior and cover.

For a previous book I'd used page numbers in the manuscript. In removing them I missed a few but fortunately they could be removed from the PDF itself. That saved me having to remove them from the book-sized big file then recreate the PDF file.

Proof approval is totally the author's responsibility. Invest the necessary time. Don't be diligent and you'll be sorry, in particular if later you hear from someone who read the book and found an embarrassing number of errors. Errors are more commonly found in publications nowadays and one or two are unlikely to upset most readers or other book buyers. More discovered...look out!

After the PDF conversion, aside from getting a book printing quotation (see above), there are other matters to consider and address—some right after the book printing, and others during the marketing process: title registration with Bowker in the U.S, registries closer to home, other exposure possibilities (local newspaper listing, professional publications). As to the latter, I got my novel cover included in one publication and a book mention in another. What about getting listed by a library services distributor? These and other such matters were dealt with in the self-publishing and are also mentioned in the next section.

Well, books in hand, what must be done to get rid of all those books printed, those that otherwise may end up piled in a corner gathering dust...

Flogging That Creation

Well, the manuscript is finally finished. Is it a job well done? Are you satisfied? If not, revise some more. Best you can do, it's time to get all those words into print, and thereafter manage to get copies into the hands of readers, perhaps eager readers with money to spend, hopefully on your creation.

Inspired and in search of a publisher? Surf the internet, ask a librarian or scan available resources on library shelves. Seek the names and contact information for firms dealing with or focusing upon your book's key topic, or its genre if a novel.

Or you might attempt to cosy up to an agent. Not an easy achievement. If you receive a response carefully consider what that contains. Agents aren't all equal. Some folk have been asked by agents to pay a reading charge, one that can range upwards of a hundred dollars. Of writers I've encountered who have paid a fee, few were satisfied with the results. If

I paid at all, and that's doubtful, I'd not pay anyone I didn't know personally or by way of an enthusiastic referral.

Paper submissions to publishers, neatly composed and bundled for sending, were once the norm. Nowadays, electronic submission is what's wanted, at least for an initial query. And, although email messages are nowadays more casual in tone and structure, that relaxed attitude cannot extend to what you send along hoping to impress a discerning stranger.

Anything short of a concise and polished submission is all but guaranteed a swift trip to the reject pile or that round receptacle occupying floor space. And, before attaching a writing sample to an email message, check to determine if the publisher would prefer the sample included within the email message itself.

Publishers, if unsolicited submissions are considered at all, won't waste staff time on shoddy material poorly presented or fraught with errors. If opening paragraphs fail to impress or a novel lacks sufficient decent dialogue, the manuscript rapidly joins the reject pile.

Querying a publisher is obviously better than not attempting to establish contact at all. But, be sure that your well-organised material, your emissary, is addressed to someone by name, a publisher or editor already determined to be interested in your writing genre or topic. Don't be boring. Be enthusiastic, upbeat and inventive. Sound confident but respectful. Start a preferably one or two page query (time is money) with something catchy and fresh. Slant the message toward the intended recipient's anticipated interests and include any writing or other applicable background credentials.

If you must later check your query's status, don't call; send a polite follow up message and accept that the person at the other end has a busy desk. If told (by email?) a submission is not of interest, ask what else could be or if there's another other firm that might be interested in what you'd submitted.

Assume that getting any kind of reply will take time. But, queries too often ignored, don't assume that no news is good news. Be patient—beyond endurance if need be. Nothing heard months later, after suitable follow up, put that failed attempt behind you and invest your energy elsewhere. A negative response received, consider any accompanying comments; could one or two prove valuable in framing future queries?

Throughout the undertaking, don't despair. The best of writers have been ignored or rejected at one time or other—some many times over. To lessen the pain, try not to get your hopes up too high at the outset. Stay positive but always be prepared for rejection or, more likely, being ignored. After a while such treatment becomes less bothersome, less a matter to be taken personally. Keep busy; send out other queries.

Years ago I used to keep reject notifications but the pile grew burdensome, so I recycled the letters, used the blank backsides for draft printing.

Publishing options vary. Those incurring no cost to a writer (a traditional publisher) are scarce and seldom easy to access. And the meaning of *publisher* has changed in recent years. While those old fashioned firms yet exist, many operations using the term no longer absorb book creation costs, have ready access to book distribution, arranged book launchings or pay royalties.

What used to be called vanity press (writer pays all) is nowadays a more obscure channel for getting a creation into print. A variety of cost-sharing schemes have evolved. Some offer website book listings. Others also offer full manuscript services: editing, PDF conversion, cover design and production. Some even pay royalties. All are prepared to print a book.

Other options better address the efforts of those able and willing to handle a larger chunk of all that's needed to end up with a decent book.

That doesn't mean that you shouldn't try to get your book published in the old fashioned way. Give it a go! Even try firms in another country, if feasible. Do you have any helpful friends with useful contacts? Don't sit back in despair. Keep at it. Try and then try again. Who knows, you might get lucky.

Books in Print (www.booksinprint.com) used to be a Canadian source of information on published books. That facility has now been combined with, shifted to, R.R Bowker in the U.S. (www.bowker.com, www.bowkerlink.com).

If you do get lucky and receive a response from a publisher, take care. Ensure that what's being offered is suitable and reasonable, that it measures up to what you are seeking, what you earlier anticipated.

If you feel you are about to land a traditional publisher, browse or purchase a book dealing with negotiating a writing contract, one that includes a standard agreement example. But, bear in mind that, for a first effort, you aren't necessarily in a strong position to negotiate. Likely, you need that publisher more than the firm needs you.

Unsuccessful in the attempt, no loss; you will have gained knowledge, learned more about the writing business. Or, having investigated the matter, tested the water, you might then decide that it's not the way for you to go, that it's time to move on and find another way to get that book out there.

When I moved to the West Coast in the mid-1990s, I tried to duplicate what I'd achieved a decade earlier in Toronto with the first book. Results for that new publisher search, eased by being able to use email and fax, were disappointing. I contacted over a hundred publishers (list compiled with the help of library resources) but got no bites, despite advising previous writing achievements: articles and a book. Realising that finding an easy home for the second novel wasn't going to happen, I bit the bullet and opted to pursue the self-publishing route.

For my second and third novels, my accounting background and book budget narrowed options. Self-publishing, doing as much of what's required as possible myself, appeared the best approach to the task. Complete the interior (including the PDF file) and provide a sketch and supporting detail for the cover.

Books in hand, I'd flog them myself. A sizeable undertaking but doable...or so I thought at the time. In fact I found the exercise satisfying but enervating. It wore me down. But, I plodded onward...

The Self-Publishing Route

Manuscript and cover organised, estimate the number of book copies wanted (what you feel you can dispose of). And, give thought to what you can afford to spend on the project, before anticipating any sales revenue. Determine an acceptable unit cost range, relative to the anticipated cover price for the book. Is the undertaking feasible?

Seek quotes and compare results, after deciding which best fits your project: traditional batch printing or POD (print on demand)? The latter is available from firms like Trafford Publishing with international operations that permit a book to be printed when and where ordered.

When requesting a price quote for a self-published book don't forget to add, to the book-size page count, any pages before and after those numbered: book synopsis, title page, a contents listing for non-fiction, author information.

How many books to initially order? Well, that'll depend upon your enthusiasm, how hard you are willing to work to dispose of inventory. A hundred may be too many, thirty too few. And, bear in mind that some will be given away, for promotional purposes or to family and friends. Also to consider: starting off with a smaller print run, despite a higher unit cost, will permit any subsequently discovered corrections or alterations to be made without having to scrap a bunch of books.

Is there a preferred time of year to publish your book, one that better accommodates its nature or targeted readers (crafts, outdoors, seasonal slant)?

A printing in January rather than December will provide a copyright date of, say, 2008 rather than 2007. Will that extend the book's life in the marketplace? For books expected to go into libraries, a late-in-year or a just-passed-yearend production date accommodates the timeframe for registering the book for Public Lending Rights (see self-publishing section).

Flogging the Books

Sales pursuits should include the expected regular channels (bookshops, libraries) plus other potential outlets (craft shops, pharmacies). Like bookshops, connecting with libraries is labour intensive, a lot of work for debatable, perhaps minimal, results, in particular without a book review to render assistance.

Being ignored is frustrating but to be expected. Yet, persistence can pay off, with approaches being rethought and altered to improve subsequent contacts. If you run out of ideas, talk to other writers in a similar position and ask them how they dispose of their books. Know anyone in the book business? Frustrated with library-accessing results, ask friends to request your book at their library branch.

An email message sent to libraries:

LIBRARY, BOOK ACQUISITIONS: Below, information regarding my third novel: Coming Up Short (305 pages, perfect bound trade, intended for adults), published in December06. Price: $17(cover); shipment prepaid in lieu of discount. GST exempt. My previous book, No More Illusions, was purchased by libraries, that included Victoria, Vancouver Island Regional, Vancouver and Toronto.

* Cover shot attached *

STORY LINE (back cover): Steve Wrift, an accountant fated to attract trouble, is fired
from a job and abandons Canada's West Coast for
employment in Australia. With travel time to
spare, he arranges a stopover in Japan to visit
a penpal. Visiting Kamakura he's given a piece
of jade by a member of the Yakuza, Japan's version of the mafia. That stone later discarded
in frustration, Steve discovers another on a
bed pillow after a night of passion in Hong
Kong. A lonely Steve, settled in Melbourne,
must deal with a vengeful female boss. While
debating limited options, he bumps into a reformed Charlie Tucker, a wastrel friend from
the past with whom Steve has shared mishaps, on
and off since they first met in Istanbul.
Checking into a company problem in Sydney,
Steve discovers more than expected. Meanwhile,
Charlie wrestles with complications arising
from a personal relationship.   .

AUTHOR: An accountant doubtlessly aspiring
to become a writer, the author—now in his
seventies and living on Vancouver Island—
abandoned senior corporate life in the mid-
seventies for consulting. Subsequent to a
first article on computers published in the
mid-1980s, over a hundred and fifty articles have appeared in several publications
and two newspaper columns. Also, some years
ago I provided computer sections for an
accounting text produced by a major publisher. To follow *Coming Up Short,* a book
on writing and one based on material accumulated from past global trips. Left to
simmer on a back burner is a limping-along

non-fiction tale about twelve years running a southern Vancouver Island farm.

Back of title page: copyright 2006 © Donald G. Wilkes <> All rights reserved <> No portion of this book may be reproduced or transmitted in any form or means whatsoever, excepting short passages for review, without the prior permission in writing from the publisher.

This novel is a work of fiction. Any resemblance between depicted characters or names, places or locales, incidents or events, entities or actual persons, living or dead, is unintentional or coincidental.

Library and Archives Canada Cataloguing in Publication
Gordon,Donald,1935-
Coming Up Short / Donald Gordon.
ISBN 0-9737633-1-0
I.Title.
PS8613.O73C65 2006 C813'.6 C2006-906016-9

Abbey Isle Publishing <> Printed in Victoria, Canada

A subsequent email message sent (subject: library, book acquisitions):

Since the East so frequently ignores Western Canada, why not better support our own? A BC writer, I want more people to read my latest novel and would appreciate your help accomplishing that. Reader response has been positive. COVER SHOT ATTACHED.

Information, Coming Up Short: 300 pages, perfect bound trade, intended for adults. Published December06. Price: $17. Shipment ($2.70 per book) prepaid in lieu of discount. GST exempt. My previous novel, No More Illusions, was purchased by libraries that included Victoria, Vancouver Island Regional, Vancouver and Toronto.

Back of title page: unchanged from previous…

Storyline (back cover): unchanged from previous…

Author: An accountant doubtlessly aspiring to become a writer, the author—now in his seventies and living on Vancouver Island—abandoned senior corporate life in the mid-seventies for consulting. Not the best move financially, doing so did provide an opportunity to pursue other interests, including writing. Subsequent to a first article on computers published in the mid-1980s (travel/other, essays to follow), over a hundred and fifty articles have appeared in publications and two newspaper columns. Also, some years back, computer sections were provided for an accounting text produced by a major publisher.

For each query (30+ days between, until acknowledgement received or I gave up) I altered the opening and to a lesser extent other content. Was the above subsequent message any better than the first? If so, how or why? If not, what would you have included, excluded? Should the first query have been more like the second?

In a later message I added a suggestion that an order be placed via their chosen library services distributor (discount expected?) and included ordering contact info to be passed along if necessary. Should that have been included in the first query?

The upper portion of the final attempt to encourage libraries to buy a book or two:

```
LIBRARY = BOOKS -> why not my book? A BC
writer, I want more people to read my lat-
est    novel.   Bought   by   BC   libraries,
I'd appreciate your help. Reader response
has been positive. My previous novel, No
More Illusions, was purchased by librar-
ies, including Victoria, Vancouver Island
Regional, Vancouver and Toronto. While I'd
rather you ordered directly, if preferable,
do place an order via your regular library
services distributor - Abbey Isle Publish-
ing, -> address <- / tks, DonW. COVER SHOT
ATTACHED. Information, Coming Up Short: 300
pages, perfect bound trade, intended for
adults. Published December06. Price: $17.
Shipment prepaid in lieu of discount. GST
exempt.
```

And...the results? Not impressive. Most libraries ignored all queries. A few acknowledged receipt, with a 'will consider.' A larger one asked for a book review (that sure disposes of hopefuls!). Few books were shipped. But in fairness, the smaller library branches are likely bound by a limited book acquisition budget, and how they choose to spend it is their business, not mine, unfortunately.

Anyway, pursuing bookshops and libraries will be frustrating, but then how or where else can books be placed, hopefully sold? The internet: how to arrange payment; are you prepared to deal with credit cards or Paypal?

No-one ever said that flogging books was easy.

As for getting books into bookshops, a labour-intensive and ever uphill battle endeavour, give some thought to focusing your efforts on less-general outlets. Try university or government bookshops, supermarkets, outlets attached to museums or other public venues attracting crowds. What about shops or organisations related to your book's genre or topic?

To better access libraries unwilling to deal with writers directly, consider contacting distribution firms, some of which may offer marketing assistance, such as The Library Services Centre, Kitchener in Ontario (www.lsc.on.ca - lscweb@lsc.on.ca, 1-800-265-3360). Expect to provide a hefty discount.

Other distributors that may contact you if requested by a library or other buyer: Coutts Library Services of Niagara Falls in Ontario (www.coutts.com, fax: 905-356-5064), United Library Services in Alberta (www.uls.com), fax: 403-258-3426). Neither of those offer a marketing (read that 'listing') service, but knowing who's out there may prove helpful in pursuing libraries (suggested alternate source?). Check the internet for others.

Read all purchase orders carefully and don't offer a discount unless requested or its mentioned as an expectation. And do pass along any mailing costs incurred.

Also be aware that shipping damage can occur. Insured postage? I declined that on the basis that accepting the odd damaged book appeared less costly than increased mailing cost to be billed, and what I'd have to go through to get any redress.

Pursuit Detail

To prepare for a direct pursuit of libraries (for me: only B.C. with a few larger possibilities eastward added) I obtained via the internet a listing and trimmed it down to name, location, fax number and email address. Since the messages to be sent were similar (occasional alteration if there was a success-ful previous contact), I sent the first message plus attached book cover shot. Next I FORWARDed that message to gain access to its content and eliminated the top portion of the message (sending details: date, sent to...). I then addressed the remaining message content for the next intended recipient on the list...and so on.

If there's no attachment to worry about, creating multiple queries within Outlook Express can also be made easier by using text capture (from the source message) and transfer (to the destination message):

- With the mouse, click/drag or FILE > SELECT ALL to highlight/select wanted text and COPY to place it on the Windows' clipboard, then use PASTE to drop the text into the onscreen destination message portion of the file.

- Or use the keyboard (hold first key down and tap second), [Ctrl]+[A] to select/highlight all and [Ctrl]+[C] to copy the selection to the clipboard. Destination message area onscreen, [Ctrl]+[V] to insert the modifying text.
- If updating a previous message sent to a library (no attachment involved), rather than bouncing back and forth between messages, you could use Notepad to hold the modifying text and move between the two opened programs by clicking on one or the other on the task bar, located at the base of the screen.

To more easily and quickly access Notepad, put it on the Desktop. Right click on the program within the START listing, drag and copy it to the Desktop.

To ease access to applications on the Desktop, arrange icons vertically, to left or right, and shift the vertical edge of any onscreen program: place the cursor on the edge to be shifted and when the double-ended arrow appears drag that edge aside to expose Desktop icons.

If you do organise and pursue a library list, update it for subsequent discoveries, such as amending email addresses that didn't work, contact names or adding any newly discovered email address (or fax numbers, if usable). Retain that list for future use. Digging into previous files (computer or hard-copy) and later trying to figure out what occurred or went amiss, is both time consuming and frustrating.

After pursuing bookshops and libraries, what next? Aside from handing out free copies, how soon will that pile of unmoved books begin to haunt you—after the dust settles? Disposing of printed copies can become an overwhelming task, in particular if you have to do it all by yourself. Keep focused and don't miss any opportunity that might arise. Seek disposal possibilities by querying family, friends, those within groups you belong to or anyone else who comes to mind.

Success doesn't come to those who sit back and wait for something to drift their way. To effectively shift those already-paid-for books, artistic inclinations must yield, in favour of adopting a businessperson's attitude. Set aside those creative aspirations for the moment and get practical. And, as some say, think outside the box.

Always be prepared to try something new. Ideas may pop up while in the midst of doing something quite apart from what revolves around that book. For example, I came across a quest in a professional publication for member authoring details. Although all the covers displayed on the page were non-fiction and business-related I immediately responded. Nonfiction or fiction, for me, an author is an author.

The cover shot and info I sent were accepted but I've yet to determine the value of that submission, but don't ask, don't get... That effort led to another quest and I got a listing in a similar publication in another province.

Persistence is all. Dig around, browse books and keep an eye out for newsletter, magazine or newspaper articles relating to shifting books. Develop a plan of attack. Pursue people and ask lots of questions. Exploit any or all contacts. Stop and review results, then press onward. Disappointed? Rethink the project. Seek another approach. Begin again.

For instance, having managed to get a self-published book announced in a local paper, I thanked the column writer, adding that all I now needed was a book review. I didn't really expect her to offer to help but why not make the attempt? Don't ask, you don't get, won't get. Few possibilities aren't worth trying, whatever the results.

Throughout the project, remember that books unsold will remain stacked in some corner, will begin to gather dust at some point. When it comes to cleaning in the past I've suggested that dust adds character—well, that doesn't apply to a book inventory. Leave no stone unturned. Soldier on and strive to come up with new ideas, other avenues you can pursue. Some may pay off and others may not. But making the attempt is what truly matters.

Exposure is important. Publicity is free. Advertising costs money.

Despite it being an uphill battle, do try to get a book review. But don't just send out books in the hope that a recipient will do a review; that's a waste of books. Query the possibility. A review in hand, even if it's not glowing, it may open a door otherwise closed to you.

Or you might try a press release. While perhaps a better bet for news rather than the publication of a book, you could get lucky and receive a positive response. Who knows? Costs little to try. That said, however, your submission will need to be fresh, focused and comprehensive, possibly brief but not too brief (3/400 words?), to get the job done. Take care with the content and layout (short paragraphs, spaced rather than indented?).

An email submission should be targeted: local radio or television shows/stations, newspapers, writing-associated publications such as BC Bookworld here in BC or other such recipients regarding fiction or non-fiction material, your genre or topic.

Should a press release go to libraries or a marketing distributor? Bookshops? Would that better catch their attention than a straight query?

What's important is to get the word out and about, particularly to those who can assist you in your endeavour. Be factual and clear. Stay on topic.

And what should an email press release contain (who, what, where, how or why?):

- Subject box: FOR IMMEDIATE RELEASE
- Below, PRESS RELEASE (with or without an asterisk or other marking either side)
- Date of the press release
- A headline: not all caps, perhaps best without exclamation marks, content that's a grabber
- Book title
- Date of publication
- Location if relevant
- A brief synopsis of the content. Something about the author and any previous successes
- If willing, specify that an interview would be welcomed
- If wished, indicate that you are seeking a review
- Add any pertinent comment, anything that would contribute value to the press release
- Contact details (name, address, phone, email)
- End the pitch with ### on the last line

An early draft of an intended press release (approx. word count: 380, email subject box: Press Release):

?? November 07
BOOK PUBLICATION
FOR IMMEDIATE RELEASE

Don't Discount or Write Off Accountants!

Title - Writing: What's Good, Bad and Ugly – Abbey Isle Publishing
Published in Victoria BC, November 2007
Number of pages - 245
Cover Price: $19

Back cover: Writing is both a simple and complex under-taking. For some it's natural and easygoing. For others it's tough slogging, a matter of being persistent, a frustrating labour of love. Write, rewrite and rewrite some more. Edit and make corrections. Review results and revise once again. Some folk manage to get polished material in a few passes. Others require extra runs through an article or manuscript. Hopefully, what you find inside will assist you in achieving a decent piece of writing, whether a short story, essay, manuscript or perhaps a self-published book ready for delivery to a printer. Sections deal with a range of writing-related topics, including ideas about getting your books into the hands of readers and handling other essential matters associated with putting pen to paper. Good luck, and hang in there. But, as is applicable to most writers, don't give up your day job...

After a preamble, the book deals with word use; short stories and articles; organising, revising, rewriting, editing and completing a manuscript; creating a book cover; self-publishing and producing a PDF file; monitoring, dispos-ing of published books and tracking item/dollar activity.

An accountant (CA) doubtlessly aspiring to become a writer, the author—now in his seventies and living on Vancouver Island—abandoned senior corporate life in the mid-1970s for consulting. Not the best move financially, doing so did provide an opportunity to pursue other interests, including writing. Subsequent to getting a first article on computers published in the mid-1980s, almost two hundred varied articles have appeared in differing publications and two newspaper columns. *Shattered Expectations*, his first novel, (as Donald Gordon) was published in 1996, to be followed by *No More Illusions* in 2005 and *Coming Up Short* in 2006. *A Bean Counter's Travels* (global trip material) is underway, as is a 1960s peek at a family's twelve years on a southern Vancouver Island farm.

The author is seeking a review and is willing to be interviewed.
Contact: name / address / phone / email address
###

Well...what do you think? Decent? Do the job? If lacking, how would you improve it?

Latching onto an opportunity to get on air or to speak at a conference could prove helpful, if you are up to that. Some innovative writers have gone to great lengths to sell their self-published books. Painting a trailer that displays your book and running all over the countryside to peddle copies won't appeal to most, but that's an example of ingenuity.

For unexpected encounters, always carry book copies in the car trunk. Recently, off for a bit of R&R, we visited one of the U.S. islands handy to Vancouver Island. Chatting with the owner of one of the bookstores, I mentioned that I was a writer and had three published books. "You should have brought books along." Wow, an opportunity! "I have some in the car. Be right back." I hustled a few blocks back to where the car was parked, grabbed the box of books and returned to the shop. She bought (not consignment) one of each and, deed done, she added a sticker to the front cover: signed by author. How's that for Boy Scout training (all of two weeks)? Be prepared! Not sure what I'll do if they sell and she wants more—how to get them there at a reasonable cost? I guess I'll just have to deal with that problem if it arises...

Network beyond other writers. Seek opportunities to wave a book about. If taking a night course, ask if the college bookstore will take a few copies. Join a writing group and perhaps sell a few books at meetings. At a party don't overdo it but do try to mention that you are a writer and that you've just written a book.

If you belong to an organisation, offer copies for prizes or try to get a mention in any newsletter.

When ordering books, get an extra copy of the cover for scanning purposes. Or arrange to have extra book covers printed on lighter stock for use in a press kit, as posters on tables at shows or fairs or as query mailers. While other possibilities may come to mind, having the book's content outlined on the back cover could prove helpful.

Ensuring that it doesn't obscure your view, why not stick a cover copy (LIBRARY? added) as a sign in your car's rear, curb-facing, window? A request at a library branch may result, may help you get a copy or two into the system.

Exploit all contacts. Arranging a financial matter at a bank, I managed to sell a book to the person I dealt with.

Attend book or craft fairs, bearing in mind they're not all equal. Select with care. I've done so and sold a few books, usually offering a special price. For one, with more copies of one book on hand, I cut the price on that one, and also offered a pair at a package price—using a multi-colour sign. Also consider other things you need to take along: books, pens, a cashbox or other receptacle, a plate stand to display the book, a black-marker, a cart for hauling the books from car to destination (if you feel that positive), sale slips (in case requested), post-its, cards or recycled business cards (back) to serve as price tags, a utility knife. What you'll take along the next time will doubtlessly be influenced by what you forgot previously.

And, don't forget to network with other writers, within your genre or not. Share experiences and discoveries. Or share tales of woe or success with others within a writing group.

Why not enter a contest or two related to your goals.

If you have access to a seniors' facility, try to arrange to read at a lunch gathering. I read an excerpt from my second novel at the seniors' centre where one of my writing groups meets. I only sold one book but I don't regret participating and will likely do so again, if only for the reading experience.

Reading what you've written aloud isn't all that easy, at least for some of us. It takes practice and writing groups are an ideal training ground. I belong to two. When I first joined, I ranked near the bottom as a reader. Nowadays, I'm not yet nudging the upper ranks but I've improved with practice, aside from a lingering inclination to read too fast. When we agreed to read at a seniors' lunch, I littered my pages with *slow* and *pause* in large red letters.

If you get lucky at a fair or a reading and manage to sell some books, what do you write if requested to sign them? Nothing but a signature. A date added. A note with the buyer's name included. Asked to do so, I'm hard-pressed to come up with something appropriate. Perhaps it's best to ask the buyer what they'd like you to write.

Remember that old saw: if you don't ask, you don't get! While self-promotion for some writers is troublesome, it is necessary, wherever and however it can be achieved: radio, television, magazines, newspapers, book-signings, newsletters...

Why not invest some research time and try schmoozing, working a potential and appropriate crowd or two. With a nametag on display? Social events. Meetings. Trade shows. Fundraisers. Reunions. Political gatherings. Appear early, meet and greet. Display a positive attitude, one pumped up and focused but not blinded by the intent. Don't interrupt, ease into a group. Eye contact and a smile do wonders, as does a firm but not crushing handshake.

Know anyone in a book club? Offer to provide a quantity of books (discounted according to the number purchased?) and attend a gathering, prepared for accolades and censure. If the venture works out, hopefully any of the latter will be more constructive than unkind. Whatever the outcome, seems a win-win situation; the group enjoys a departure from normal routine and you obtain feedback and, assuming you have taken some along, a chance to sell other books.

Why not contact a college-level teacher heading up an English literature or writing course. Again, subject to a quantity of books purchased, volunteer to appear at a student seminar. If the offer is accepted, you'll be a real live author for the students to pounce upon. I've yet to try this but I intend to do so soon, using a previous book but carrying along this one in case I get to sell a few copies after the session.

How about a community television station or an appropriate website?

Does a daily or community newspaper periodically devote some space to books? If so, are brief reviews of self-published books included? I pursued this and got mentioned in a column.

If you have any writing credentials (articles, previous books) exploit them. Include details in any press kit/release or other publicity methods used. For instance, long before I turned to writing books and had my first novel published, I'd seen well over a hundred of my articles printed. And I'd made very good money contributing computer sections for an accounting text. With more articles added to the count (to date almost two hundred in print), I certainly added those facts in the draft press release appearing earlier in this section.

For friends and members of writing groups, I always take a couple dollars off the cover price, another dollar, perhaps, if the individual bought the previous book. What's left is more profitable than what remains after giving a bookshop or library distribution service an expected discount.

A book that cost, say, twelve dollars and sells for eighteen dollars (not much margin there) isn't likely to yield the cover price a year or two after publication. That's how all those inexpensive remainders arrive in discount shops. Recognise that diminishing value and be flexible. At a craft fair, for a previous novel, I made up a Show Special sign and offered the book for ten dollars, a figure below my original cost but perhaps more than the book's worth at that point in time. For details on yearend book inventorying valuation, see section on monitoring activity.

When I got my second (first self-published) novel printed I ordered a few too many copies and the pile in the corner disturbed me, and then bothered me some more. I sweetened the new-book offer to individuals: both novels for a figure that heavily discounted the older book.

Why not create an attractive invoice, with a bit of clipart or a sketch added. Clearly display contact details. If billing the latest book, mention others below on the form. The section on monitoring activity offers invoice-structuring details.

In short, any or all book-marketing attempts, no matter the degree of success, are worth the time investment and each one represents a learning experience.

Bookshops

See if a bookshop is willing to put on a book-signing session, say two or three hours on a Saturday. Rather than buying books at a hefty discount from me, one larger bookshop provided a table at the entry door for an afternoon, with all book-sale proceeds to be retained by me. Books I displayed on the table included a handout: earlier highlights that contributed to the manuscript portions of this book. Interesting as that exercise proved to be, I didn't sell many books.

Bookshops are high maintenance, in particular the smaller ones: large discount, contact and delivery effort and time, consignment and book monitoring, unsold books retrieval, gas, shoe sole wear and tear.

Leaving a book for consideration (get a signature?) might ease the introduction; that copy to be retrieved or left on consignment. Leave one of those created invoice blanks for contact information, perhaps with notes added: date published (if relevant), discount offered (40%), 'on consignment' (if so), any other relevant details.

Many outlets, in particular the larger ones, prefer to buy their books from a book distributor. Check out that potential means of distribution? Discounting off-putting?

Some shops may appear too small to bother with. Others may only handle used books or specialise in a genre. One shop may not want to shelve your book while another willingly supports local writers. Only a visit will establish the situation.

Expect delayed decisions, yes or no. Start early and hustle to get your books out there. Then be patient, wait a month or two before following up on books left on consignment. Always be polite, even if provoked. You need the shop owner or manager more than (s)he needs you.

Something helpful discovered in one situation, consider or adapt it for another.

Monitor books left for consideration or on consignment.

Pursue payments due and overdue.

Later, visit and retrieve unsold books.

As for initially visiting bookshops, you could phone ahead but appearing in person may be more effective, more productive. Turning you down over the telephone or by email is easier than in person.

Without an appointment, multiple visits may be needed to catch the shop manager or owner in. Contact managed, be prepared for disappointment but forge onward. And bear in mind, books left on consignment and later collected may exhibit some degree of wear and tear—future giveaways?

No matter the effort involved and assorted disappointments, you need to be able to respond if or when asked where your book can be found.

Economics 101

How to price your book? Assume for the moment that anything over $20.00 is too much to ask for a self-published book from an unknown author, one with limited exposure. Scan bookshelves for similar books: novel or not, of a size, published same year or within one year, comparable cover treatment.

My first novel, published by a Toronto firm in 1996 was priced at $12.95. The next one, more pages and self-published in 2005, I priced at $17.95. The third, similar in size and a year later: $17. I could have priced the following book at $18 but chose to drop the ninety-five cents (a means to obscure gouging another buck from a reader?). For this book, fewer pages than my novels, but a self-help guide: $19. All under $20, but is that a correct approach to the matter? Should this one, because of its nature, have been priced higher?

Where's the income? For many writers it's more a case of reducing losses. Using my second novel as an example, deducting 40% (standard for a bookshop) from a $17.95 selling price left me with something under $11, roughly my unit cost, before considering expenses such as wrapping paper, postage, car costs, table rentals at craft fairs, necessary or advantageous book giveaways, computer use and supplies.

Selling books is certainly not a win-win undertaking—is, for many writers, more of a never-win enterprise. But most of us forge onward anyway. Perhaps it's a mind quirk, some warped sense of reality or what's proper and not.

Anyway, being retired and with time to invest, I wave books at friends and others, pursue libraries, bookshops and attended book fairs, expecting little more than being able to recoup some of the investment made, being able to put that book to bed so I can get on with another one. Reasonable? Probably not. Certainly doesn't sound reasonable, but I've concluded that the positives outweigh the negatives; that finally getting a new book in my hand provides sufficient compensating satisfaction.

Monitoring Activity

Writers with aspirations beyond a hobby approach to writing should keep track of all that transpires, for reasons of curiosity or necessity. What goes out and what comes in. Material shipped or delivered. Income. Expenditures. For books or articles, they need to know what was sent to whom and when, and what next occurred. Communication. Material. Dollars.

Monitoring articles or manuscript traffic could represent no more invested effort than pinning individual notes to a bulletin board, with subsequent actions to be added to the notes. Contact, by voice, letter or email query. Reactions. Material or book mailings. Follow up and comments.

For an expanded undertaking, something more elaborate may better serve. Why not a listing (with or without attached communication copies) that, at a glance, reflects for several contacts all that unfolds—whether directly related, unexpected or otherwise useful. Items sent. Comments or payments received. Other interest expressed. Responses may trigger a publicity or referral idea.

Individual notes or listings serve two purposes. They offer a record of what has happened in the past and perhaps trigger needed subsequent attention. For articles, a list provides a handy means to ensure that the mailing of material isn't duplicated, that similar items aren't sent to rival participants in the same marketing area.

Capturing the attention of an editor/publisher isn't easy and the last thing you want is to ruin an established relationship by having something printed by a competing publication within the same time period.

Decades ago in Toronto I suffered that embarrassment. That I hadn't been paid for one or both articles didn't lessen the awkwardness of the situation. The relationships survived but I'd certainly erred. Lesson learned, I never repeated that mistake.

To keep track of articles sent out I created an Excel spreadsheet (handy for any document using columns):

- The first column contained contact info: publication, location, rates paid, email address, contact person, any notation about avoiding duplication.
- Columns to the right contained details of what was sent and when, receipt reactions and payments received.

- Penciled additions or notes made to the list, messy as they became, were incorporated on subsequent printings.

To free up space for additions, that listing was at one point divided between active and dormant contacts (some response but...).

Tracking the Dollars

While I have an accounting background, and do my own bookkeeping, other folk may not be so inclined. What follows is intended to outline what's involved so you can decide if or how you wish to deal with the chore. For good reason, in what follows, you'll encounter references to talking to an accountant. That's for good reason. Regulations change and one perspective may disagree with another, may not accommodate evolving conditions or a particular responsibility situation.

Taxation aspects of a writing venture may not be overly complex but having an initial chat with an accountant sure beats spending a chunk of time browsing guidelines and regulations, perhaps having to later do battle with taxation authorities.

One way or another writing earnings are taxable and are to be reported annually. Better safe than sorry. Be meticulous in keeping track of writing income and related expenses.

Be clear in your own mind about all that's needed for the venture and then determine how to acquire, sort out or assemble the bits and pieces. Mundane related detail must be organised: working space with a telephone handy, computer selection or adaptation, communications (email, fax, maybe a website), storage space for any book inventory and supplies.

Fringe or pertinent expenditures should be evaluated; for example, revenue expected, how much should or can be spent realistically on travel or promotion. Going on a trip from which an article will result (one likely to be sold), what share of the expenses should be charged against income? Expecting my wife to contribute a perspective, I assume that three people are involved: the two of us, and a third that represents the article for its share of relevant costs.

Self-publishing books is a business, as is writing articles if notable earnings accumulate. If still working: a part time effort. If retired, the undertaking could dominate your time, or perhaps it should do so if significant earnings are a distinct possibility.

More casual writing (not organised as a publishing entity, perhaps a proprietorship) generally permits defined expenses to be deducted from present or future writing income only. Any loss in a year cannot be deducted from other income but can be carried forward into future years.

Registering a publishing proprietorship for producing books permits a bit more latitude but any expense allocation for use of home space cannot be claimed in any one year beyond income that accommodates the deduction—a loss (to claim against other income) cannot be created by applying a share of household costs.

For clarification on the issue, obtain a Canadian Revenue Agency (CRA, 'tax department') brochure containing the related forms: T777, IT525.

To get some idea of where you are headed and how you expect to get there, consider creating an initial budget on a columnar pad or by using a spreadsheet program such as Excel. Enter estimates of expected revenue, anticipated space costs, computer and supplies, travel and promotion, book costs, postage, other categories and miscellaneous. Amend the budget as you move ahead, adding or deleting items or categories. For a clearer perspective of categories involved, obtain a CRA small business brochure (GST details included), here in Victoria on Vancouver Street.

Assuming that having a publisher's name on the book cover and title page of a self-published book has value—both for the book's appearance and acceptance, perhaps taxation status—you may wish to create your own publishing label. In Victoria details and forms to arrange a sole proprietorship are available from the Ministry of Finance, located by the downtown central library branch. Before heading there, have three diverse names (the more unusual, the better) in mind. No luck with those three, another name search will bear added cost. If you do establish a publishing label, within the book refer to yourself (as author) in the third person (John Smith or he, rather than I).

Should you register a publishing proprietorship and be tempted to publish someone else's book, take care. Family or close friends involved: differing understanding as to what is involved, unappreciated invested effort, a potential for arising dispute. As to

219

the content, is there any possible exposure to libel or other discomforting or serious implications? Being responsible for what you do is one thing; being responsible for what someone else writes is another.

If you establish a proprietorship for the enterprise using a name other than your own (and why not?) and don't wish to maintain a separate business bank account for a lesser number of arriving cheques, carefully structure your invoice so that cheques are to be made payable to you, not to the chosen publishing name. After all, a proprietorship is not an incorporated company—it's a division of you, and as such represents another source of income that you're responsible for reporting annually on a tax return.

A business bank account bears monthly charges (ten dollars a month, more?). For minimal sales, who needs added cost and record keeping? If the odd cheque arrives in the proprietorship name and attempts to get it altered fail, the loss to you will still be less than charges imposed for a business bank account. If, or as, the enterprise expands a business account could then be reconsidered.

Whatever you decide to do, it's best to run your intentions by an accountant.

While selling articles to newspapers or magazines is unlikely to require a billing, shipping books will. Fortunately these days there's no need to run out and buy a bundle of stylized invoices. For more modest needs, purchase from a stationery shop a ready-made pad (one plus a copy) of sales slips with boxed space at the top for adding billing and contact information. Something more elaborate preferred or required? Create an attractive invoice on a computer, one that combines fonts in differing sizes and maybe includes a sketch, bit of clipart or picture that relates to the enterprise.

Examine invoices you come across to gather content ideas. For your billing, specify book title, number of copies being purchased, discount percentage deducted, net price, shipping basis and GST billing or status (exempt?). An example, layout and spacing adjusted as needed for appearance:

- (upper left, for you) Billed by and Payable to:
  -name-, -address-, -address-, -postal code-,
  -phone number-, -email address-
- (upper middle) a bit of clipart, a logo, a picture of some sort
- (upper right) Billing Date:
- (upper right, next below, for purchaser) Billed to:
  -name-, -address-, -address-, -address-,
  -postal code-
- (upper right, next below) Billing Due/Payable When Rendered (or other terms)
- _____ (across form, to separate top from body)
- (invoice body) # Book(s): -book name-, -ISBN #-, -$cover price-
- Less   % discount = -$bill price-   (to right)
- +Prepaid postage   -$cost-   (to right)
- GST status (exempt?)   ---------   (to right)
- ·   -$total-   (to right)
- ·   =======   (to right)
- _____ (across form, to separate body from lower)
- Purchase order to -proprietor name-,
  -PO number-, -date-

221

Full-page invoice or a half-page one? It the latter and you wish to add another bar/line across the bottom for appearance, make sure that in doing so (as for any other alterations) the document length doesn't exceed one-half the page. If space becomes a bit tight, narrow the page margins, FILE > PAGE SETUP (inches): top/.9, bottom/.5, sides/.5, header –footer/0.

If adopting a two-up approach, within MS Word, having already created an invoice blank template with only one invoice on it. Open that template and FILE > SAVE AS it under a name that reflects the recipient and billing specifics. Contrary to Windows largess, I use four letters to identify the buyer, add a digit for year and then three letters for the month (BBBB7MMM), but then I'm an old DOS-conditioned guy: eight characters for a filename, maximum.

Billing details completed, select/highlight the content and copy/paste it to the bottom half of the page to provide that needed file copy. If an overlap to a second page occurs, don't save the altered form.

Abandon the file and return to what was saved after completing the top invoice form. Adjust the layout for a fit (remove any last line across added?) and if necessary, amend the invoice template accordingly.

Problem sorted, repeat the copy to the lower half of the page. All as it should be, for a clean page division, neatly separate billing copies using a metal edged ruler and a sharp blade.

If there's another billing to the same buyer in a month, copy a previous billing and FILE > SAVE AS it, adding a '2' or '3' to the end of that filename. Then carefully amend what differs for this billing.

For books sold I prepay any postage and include the cost on the invoice (amount charged based upon a similar previous shipment). Most orders received for one book, I shipped one three-book order separately wrapped to reduce the postage cost/charge and also to lessen the chance of in-transit wrapping damage (weight, books shifting as package tossed about).

Aside from postal cost implications, do otherwise consider paper thickness. Thinner pages in a book feel better and ease handling for reading. On the other hand, if the number of book pages is going to produce a too-slim volume, consider fattening up the book a bit with heavier paper.

What about an additional handling charge? For many purchases these days that seems a popular means for extracting a few added billing dollars. Though I do not impose such a charge, I've been asked if I do. Tempted? Ask around to see if anyone else is doing it.

Do your books differ in thickness? A modest adjustment to 'shipping' could be used to compensate for the difference between a book that'll fit through the postal slot and another that won't. The postage cost for my third novel was $2.70, considerably less than what I paid for the previous thicker book. Would charging $3.60 for both be fair, help to recover some of the excess postage for the fatter book? Would that be acceptable to a book buyer?

Save additional postage and an envelope, perhaps shorten the payment interval, by enclosing invoices within books shipped and specifying that fact on the outside of the wrapping ('invoice enclosed').

For your records, attach an invoice copy to the purchase order and anything else related to that book order.

For books you deliver—left for payment or on consignment—get a signature on the invoice copy to be retained by you.

Bookshops and some distributors will expect a 40% discount. Larger book outlets or distributors may expect something larger. Take care in determining what's fit and proper, compared to what's expected. Why give away more than necessary.

Don't offer a discount if there's no indication that one is expected. A purchase order received, read it carefully and use the content to guide discounting. Wording may indicate that the maximum provided to any customer is what's expected. For me, that's 40%.

To ease book-billing calculations, create a net-of-discount-range schedule (computer spreadsheet?) based upon cover price minus 10%, 15%, 20% -> 40% discount. Use those net figures per book on invoices. The lower percentages, if used at all, will apply to any courtesy discount allotted.

Carry created blank invoices or a sales pad (contact info added) and a discount sheet with you when visiting bookshops in case you need to produce an instant billing, perhaps one noted as consignment. Why bill later and pay the postage? My penmanship is awful but scribbled invoices have been accepted, albeit with an odd stare sent my way.

As a writer earning income, you are expected to report income from that source on your annual tax return. Short stories. Articles. Books. Given a reasonable expectation of income in the not-too-distant future, related expenditures can be deducted, within the revenue produced, or beyond under some circumstances or conditions. Talk to an accountant or obtain a CRA brochure (pick up, request or via the internet) regarding expense deductibility.

Expectation as to income is the key word, assuming a realistic passage of time. Writing a bit here and there, dealing with writing as a hobby is less likely to qualify. Additional factors that may reinforce qualification: printed article copies, books in print, writing-related documentation, a record of marketing effort, correspondence, documented successful involvement, participation of a publisher, related memberships.

For proper bookkeeping, you'll need to keep track of income and expenses—or pay someone else to do so. In the interest of cost savings, early on obtain some guidance information. To reduce expense, try to do as much of what's necessary yourself. A wide columnar pad or a spreadsheet program works well for keeping track of modest income and expenses (see below).

And what expenses can be claimed against writing income? Basically: book printing costs, supplies and copying, a share of auto costs (recorded kilometres at a rate per?), applicable memberships, accounting or legal fees, applicable equipment (as depreciation?) and repairs, postage, related travel, delivery costs, appropriate writing-related meals (a portion). A share of household costs relating to dedicated office space (based upon the number of rooms or a percentage of total floor space) may also qualify.

If operating expenses can be claimed on your annual tax return, bear in mind that the household cost portion (as calculated: room/floor space) is only deductible in any one year if there's sufficient revenue to accommodate it (see CRA Business and Professional Income brochure for details). As for meals, any appropriate entertainment or meeting deduction is limited to fifty-percent of what was paid. I've always wondered if that ruling also applies to those making the regulations or otherwise working within the halls of government...

Keeping proper and complete records, accounts, is important, is the key to successfully dealing with the CRA should the occasion arise. Careful and tidy bookkeeping backed up with billing and expenditure documents. Although there are many more taxpayer submissions than taxation auditors, you never know when a random check may occur or an unrelated error on your tax return may initiate an audit. Be meticulous. Be prepared.

If anticipated annual revenue is less than $30,000, should you register for GST? Some say yes and others no. If you do not register you do not have to bill GST for sales but cannot claim GST paid for writing-related expenditures. The latter is a simpler operating mode but then people may be aware of your maximum annual revenue, if that matters. It doesn't to me, but then I'm a retired guy.

Read the GST regulations carefully and if in doubt run the matter by someone knowledgeable and ensure that (s)he is aware of your situation or any unusual circumstances.

Billing for books is one thing. Collecting the funds is another. Pursuing overdue receivables is important, is sometimes that may need doing unless you're prepared to forego the dollars billed. Most folk pay within a reasonable span of time, but there are always a few that need a polite nudge or two, perhaps something more blunt in later days.

My invoices specify that billings are due and payable upon receipt. Getting paid within thirty days is acceptable. For one purchaser I have to consistently send an email message to get paid within ninety days. Unacceptable. I pursued the matter and managed to get my billing payment term reduced from their usual 60 days to 30. Better, but...

Records

While there are admirable computer-based accounting programs available (Quicken is popular), do they represent overkill for most writers, in particular for those experiencing modest activity? Do you need such a program? Bear in mind that to use one you must first invest some measure of program-learning time.

For writing purposes, I created an income and expense tracking spreadsheet resembling (squashed for a fit):

WRITING: INCOME AND EXPENSES FOR YEAR: 2007

DATE/DETAILS/WRITER/REVENUE/SPACE/COMP/TRAVEL/POST/MISC-detail					SUPP	PROM	OTHER	
01jan open.figs	-250						250	books
23jan lunch	-13				13			
12feb rev.sheet	240	-240						
23mar cash trans	-120			60	55	5		
~ ~ ~ ~ ~ ~ ~ ~ ~ ~								
31dec space/yr	-500		500					
31dec comp/yr	- 400			400				
31dec travel	- 30				30			
	-1073	-240	500	460	98	5	250	

227

At least for those early days, a columnar pad not suited, why not create such a computer spreadsheet (aka worksheet) to track transactions. Year completed, adjust income and expense totals for any significant yearend unpaid billings or expenditures (accruals). Sound too complicated or not appealing to you? Time to talk to that accountant.

If operating a separate bank account for writing transactions, you may wish to keep the records in dollars and cents, at least for the bank column (replaces 'writer' above).

But wider columns will decrease the number of possible distribution columns that'll fit within a sheet printed landscape (sideways).

To combine using dollars and cents for the first column and dollars only for others, consider adding to the spreadsheet a narrow 'cents elimination' column and formula. I started out this way but later decided to simplify the task. I don't keep a separate bank account for writing and do my 'books' in whole dollars (as above), rounding entries to the nearest dollar, with whole dollar totals used on my annual tax return.

Assuming that a worksheet is what you'll use, create a blank template that'll only be used for copying as needed for use. Beyond opening entries (items carried forward from previous year) appearing on the first row or line, the template should include lines for space usage and a share of computer use (if system personally owned), auto expense (kilometres @ rate per?) and any yearend book inventory.

To create, say, *Books07-1,* use FILE > SAVE AS on that created template. If or when a sheet is filled and another's needed, access the blank template and use it to create another worksheet for use, this one saved it as *Books07-2.* Carry column totals from the first sheet forward as the first row/line of the second sheet.

Alternately, where one worksheet will suffice for a year, to prepare an entry sheet for a following year, FILE > SAVE AS *Books07 to Books08* and delete entries and other content unneeded for the new year.

If you don't use a comprehensive file computer backup routine, back up worksheets to a floppy disk, rewritable CD/DVD or a USB/flash drive. Or, that not appealing, print sheets after adding transactions and retain the latest sheet in case it's needed to recreated what has transpired.

Assuming there's no separate bank account for writing, for a line/row entry, anything recorded in the WRITER column is offset by an entry or entries elsewhere on the sheet. Positive upfront (received, what you owe), negative elsewhere. Negative upfront (paid out, what you're owed), positive elsewhere.

Use distribution columns for the most-active categories such as revenue and supplies, with occasional-use items being entered in the far right column, MISC, with a brief identifying notation to the right.

Spreadsheet Use (GST ignored)

Opening figures: At the start of a new year, if a bank account is maintained for writing alone, the opening bank balance is entered: positive in the bank column, negative way over in the MISC column with 'bank' noted to the right. Other opening figures, entered in the first column and elsewhere as applicable, could include such items as books unsold during the year previously or unusually large-dollar-value supplies on hand. In other words, notable items not totally expensed in the year before. For books, consider reducing the cost-based value of those unsold at yearend, increasingly so as each year passes.

Billings issued: As billings are made, retain the file copy in a pending file. As paid, bundle and list the invoice copies on a sheet for entry, along with any unbilled revenue (articles?) received. Activity determining recording frequency for summary sheets: a positive figure in the first column, a negative in the revenue column. Once the summary sheet is recorded, store it and attachments in a 'completed transaction' envelope/box.

Expenses paid: Stow unpaid invoices in a pending file until paid and entered: negative in the first column, positive as applicable for distribution. Credit card slips or cash-paid chits for lesser outlays such as copying costs, minor supplies, self-help books, postage stamps, taxi fares could be kept on a paper-spike or otherwise retained until bundled and recorded. Enough gathered, list them on a sheet by category. To record the items, enter the total negative in the first column and the column distribution as positive figures. Date and store the list and attachments in the 'completed transactions' envelope/box.

Adjustments: From time to time an adjustment may be required. For example, an entry error on a previously printed page is discovered or an expense allocation decision subsequently changes. Adjustments seldom involve the first column. For instance, say, on a previous sheet, an expense amount ended up in the travel column by mistake. That positive figure in the travel column is removed by entering an equivalent negative figure there and then a positive figure in the proper column with 'allocation correction' noted in the details column.

Prepaid expense: For whatever valid reason you might decide that a substantial outlay (promotion brochure, books, extraordinary supplies expenditure) should be should be expensed over more than one year, rather than when the bill was paid. If a portion hasn't already been set aside in the far right column, at the yearend enter that amount as a negative in the distribution column where it was recorded and as a positive figure in the MISC column with a notation to the right. Unsold books are more an inventory than a prepaid expense but are dealt with the same way. Count and value books for sale according to longevity and apply a realistic valuation. For example, for a book that's not a long-living winner and assuming an initial cost of $11, why not devalue unsold units: $8 at the end of the following year, $5 for the next and then $3.

Capital outlays: Purchasing more significant items (see taxation guidelines for details) such as computer gear and what it sits upon, the cost involved may or may not be permitted as an expense in the year acquired, may involve depreciation at rates set by CRA. Consider purchasing a computer personally and allocating a portion of the cost (as non-personal use) to the writing enterprise. This topic is a good one to run by an accountant.

Shared costs: As a small business venture (a sole proprietor?), working at home is both practical and less costly, with or without a mailbox address used. With a room set aside for writing, appropriate household costs can in part be expensed, based upon the best calculation: number of rooms or a percentage of floor space. Qualifying expense items include rent or taxes, mortgage interest, communications, heating, lighting, maintenance and household insurance. Depreciation on the house is best not charged as doing so can create a taxable gain as a result of a later property sale. For auto use, keeping track of applicable kilometres and applying a rate per kilometre (up to last government rate used?) may be the easiest way to allocate what it costs to run and maintain an automobile.

Are the books in balance? In the spreadsheet I use I added, bottom right hand corner, a formula and in-balance indicator that, after each entry, should always be a zero. If the cross-foot total isn't zero the worksheet is out of balance and errors must be corrected before carrying forward any column totals to a new page.

I've used spreadsheets for many years, but not in an overly complicated way. Excel is the most popular worksheet program today but it certainly wasn't the first such utility. VisiCalc, I believe, was the first, that to be followed by Quattro, Lotus123 and perhaps others. Each later program version improved upon the one that preceded it. To apply formulas to spreadsheets you'll need to get a self-help guide to augment what can be gained by tapping the [F1] key for focused help. Or, you may wish to seek guidance via the internet. Use Google or other search engines to access related websites. Enter *excel+formula* or another word combination to narrow or better define your quest.

For those comfortable with their situation or who have checked with an accountant and plan to do their own annual tax returns, an example of an Income & Expense Statement (notes to right: info only), one that, meals aside (included in 'travel' as 'promotion'), should provide details needed for completing the annual tax return schedule (T2124):

Income/Expense Statement for > name <
Year ended, 31 December 07

Income		2000	> could be more than one category
Expenses:			
Space	500		> check MISC for expense or
Supplies	200		income items to be listed .
Travel	150		(not items like 'books' to
Sundry	100		be carried forward)
	-----	950	
Net Income		$1050	

Figures appearing in the above report can be obtained by having transaction totals in the worksheet feed a report framed below. My template is set up that way: books above, report below. When I wish to print the 'books' or 'report' I select/highlight that portion and print just that.

Resources

There is no shortage of how-to books, self-help offer-ings, but as applicable to anything else, some help-mates are better than others, better address the assistance required, whatever the quandary. Short story or essay. A chosen genre. Fiction or non-fiction. Structure. Dialogue. Some books written by success-ful authors work well and do prove helpful; others don't. But then, how better to get an idea of what's needed than to browse the works of those who have achieved a measure of success at the craft.

So, don't rush into a bookshop and indiscrimi-nately buy any topical book with a fetching cover or title. Open the book. Examine the contents listing. Browse a chapter or two. If provided, check the au-thor's credentials. Satisfy yourself that you'll get your money's worth; that a sizeable portion of the book will address your issue.

Many of the helpmates I have on my shelves (couple dozen or so) were purchased in Toronto and carried west. Some came from larger outlets. Others I found on clearance counters. A few were gifts. Those added here in Victoria were discovered in smaller shops, garage sales and book disposals such as the massive annual Times Colonist undertaking to raise funds for literacy. A worthy cause, I've contributed boxes of books.

Visit libraries and other book sources. It's surprising what turns up, including the odd gem. What follows is a partial list of books I've acquired and retained through the years. No doubt there are many others that are worthy, some perhaps even better than those I possess. Anyway, those I have tend to focus on specific aspects of writing and they've proven helpful, at one time or other, to one extent or another. I've received little benefit from more general books on writing.

Helpful material can also be found in writing-related magazines, newsletters and items that might get circulated at writing groups. Gather it all up and tuck it away in a file, to be browsed from time to time in search of something for a current project. If you're the last one to read a magazine that contains save-able information, and it's all right to do so, tear out pages. It's amazing what accumulates over the years, and how handy some of it proves to be.

Before all else: a superior dictionary and thesaurus. Both bulky. I keep an Oxford dictionary and Collins thesaurus parked by a comfortable chair where I often do hardcopy revisions. Handy to the computer: Webster's New World's heavy-duty dictionary and thesaurus.

Not far away (for grammar and such nitty-gritty): *A Writer's Handbook Of Current English*, Michael D.

Moore, Gage Educational (Canadian); *The Canadian Style*, Department of the Secretary of State of Canada; *The Modern Writer's Handbook*, Frank O'Hare and Edward A. Cline, Macmillan Publishing (US).

Less frequently consulted (a formidable undertaking): *Fowler's Modern English Usage* (Oxford Press).

Also found on my shelf: *On Writing Well* by William Zinsser and that tiny gem, *Elements of Style* by William Strunk Jr and E.B. White.

Why multiple reference resources? Some troublesome items are better covered in one book than another.

There are hordes of writing reference books out there and most of those that reside on my shelf have contributed something to improving my writing efforts. Some may be getting a bit long in the tooth but they remain relevant, age seemingly of lesser importance with such books. What's needed is to have on hand the right helpmates, for when they're needed. Keep an eye out and add new discoveries, perhaps disposing of those that have failed to measure up. On reflection, if initially I'd invested a bit more browsing time, I mightn't have bought a few of those I did.

Among those listed below, ones I found particularly helpful: *How To Write Realistic Dialogue*, Jean Saunders, Allison & Busby; *Conflict, Action & Suspense*, William Noble, Writer's Digest Books; *Self-Editing For Fiction Writers*, Renni Browne and Dave King, Harper Perennial.

Some to consider (topics rather than actual books?):

- *How To Write Realistic Dialogue*, Jean Saunders, Allison & Busby
- *Dialogue*, Lewis Turco, Writer's Digest Books

Of the two, I found the former more helpful but the latter added perspective.

- *Conflict, Action & Suspense*, William Noble, Writer's Digest Books
  To quote the author: What makes a story interesting? What hold a readers attention? What rivets eyes to the page and feeds an urge for more and more and more...

- *The First Five Pages*, Noah Lukeman, A Fireside Book
  The importance of early book pages to readers. The book also covers a range of manuscript topics.

- *The Joy Of Writing Sex*, Elizabeth Benedict, Story Press
- *Writing Erotic Fiction*, Mike Bailey, Teach Yourself Books
  Both offered suggestions and examples. Another book I found helpful: Delta of Venus, Erotica by Anaïs Nin, a novel.

- *Getting The Words Right*, Theodore A Rees Cheney, Writer's Digest Books
  Sub-text: how to rewrite, edit and revise.

- *Self-Editing For Fiction Writers*, Renni Browne and Dave King, Harper Perennial
  Covers: show and tell, characterisation, point of view, dialogue, interior monologue, proportion, etc.

- *Revising Fiction*, David Madden, a Plume Book
  One hundred and eighty-five practical techniques for improving your story or novel.

- *A Passion For Narrative*, Jack Hodgins, McClelland & Stewart
  A guide for writing fiction, the award-winning novelist and short story writer preaches what he practices, gets into a range of writing topics: setting, character, Plot, etc.

- *Is There A Book In You?* Dan Poynter & Mindy Bingham, Para Publishing
  The basics and mechanics of authoring a book are presented, as well as related matters. Check Dan Poynter's website for other helpful material and books: www.parapublishing.com.

- *The Weekend Novelist*, Robert J Ray, Bell Trade
  Focusing on part-time writing, the book delves into aspects of the craft.

- *What If?* Anne Bernays and Pamela Painter, Harper Perennial
  A group of writing exercises for fiction writers: beginning, story elements, characterisation, dialogue, plot, etc.

- *Negotiating A Book Contract*, Mark L Levine, Moyer Bell Limited.

- *How To Murder A Naked Lady*, Eliza Hemingway, Arts Angels Publishing

If you expect others to be attracted to your work, what you write must first matter to you. A lot! Your fiction creation should produce word pictures, tantalising images, if you expect to entice a potential book buyer. There are oodles of books out there, each competing for attention, attempting to grab that passing reader, entice her or him into digging out some cash or plastic.

Putting together a book, combining all the bits and pieces into a finished product, could be compared to assembling and decorating a model. Words the pieces, structure and style represent the glue and paint. But differing with writing, after assembly and a measure of embellishment, you're not done; work remains.

What's been written must be scrutinized and then again, expanded or reduced, taken apart or rearranged with sentences or paragraphs shifted about. And, all that's before final tidy-up and polishing, and all that must be done thereafter, such as conversion for printing, marketing and monitoring what later transpires.

Truthfully, a book is never really finished—rewriting only stops when you feel totally drained or, a massive effort invested, can no longer stand the sight of the manuscript. And that's more than likely to happen.

808.02 Gordo

Gordon, D.
Writing.

PRICE: $20.56 (3559/he   )

This book is dedicated to my friend Don McInnis, a savvy guy who contributed to its content, directly in proofreading and improving what appeared on paper (my thanks) and indirectly through our numerous writing-related exchanges. Subsequent revisions occurring, any residual errors are all mine. Over the years we've debated word use and pronunciation, the accomplishments of scribes and contributions to the world of music. We've also deplored a few political issues and those associated with them. A dictionary-browsing enthusiast, for fiction, he's a staunch William Faulkner fan while I favour Wilbur Smith.

Novels as Donald Gordon:

Shattered Expectations
No More Illusions
Coming Up Short

An odd combination: novel and autobiography, with how-to suggestions that stray from what's normally belaboured.

Another book on writing I found interesting was one I picked up at a garage sale: *The Mother Tongue, English & How It Got That Way*, Bill Bryson, William Morrow And Company. The first book from that author I read was *In A Sunburnt Country*, Random House Of Canada, a delightful exposure to portions of Australia off the tourist-beaten path. It proved helpful in with my third novel and in assembling an article on Australia. Another of his books I have: *Notes From A Small Island*, McClelland & Stewart (a tour of the United Kingdom).

Anyway, *The Mother Tongue...*, for those interested, along with dealing with the world dominance of the English language, the author covers pronunciation, spelling, swearing and other wordplay. He also delves into the dawn of language and the sources of words. An interesting read without doubt and it offers a bonus: seven pages of selected bibliography.

Books on self-publishing of particular interest? And why not, for those pursuing that path. Browse potential helpmates before digging out the cash or plastic. Or, check the internet for content comment or a review. Or, seek other potential helpmates on the web. Available: *The Self-publishing Manual*, Dan Poynter; *Self Publishing in Canada*, Suzanne Anderson, *Self-Publishing for Dummies*, Jason R. Rich.

Seeking Information

Not all that long ago, information was sought from and unearthed in libraries. The benefits that flowed from such searches depended upon the quantity and quality of books found on the shelves. While that source remains valuable, more and more pertinent data are now obtained from websites found on the internet. Despite debatable material cluttering up cyberspace, research has become faster and easier. The focus has shifted from trying to find what's needed to how to reduce the information overload and separate out what's required.

Recently I visited the downtown library branch here in Victoria and browsed the shelves containing writing-related books (800-808). There were lots of books there but I didn't find any of mine, those I'd found so helpful. Perhaps I should consider donating what I have so others can share the benefits I've enjoyed. But, funds expended, can I get a tax deduction for such a donation?

Anyway, I scanned titles on the library's shelf, and withdrew the odd book to check content. Several books appeared to have suffered years of handling (or not). Then I came upon one that surprised me—a recent book on writing humour. Wow! That was a topic I'd pursued on the internet with minimal results. The book discovered: *Comedy Writing Secrets*, Mel Helitzer + Mark Swatz, Writer's Digest Books.

Cyberspace is a marvellous source of information, as long as you're prepared to invest the time and effort. To ferret out what you seek, there's a host of debatable material to wade through. Using Google, Yahoo, Alta Vista or another web search engine,